D15674731

STAGE DESIGN

BY RALPH LARMANN

daab

INTRODUCTION

Modern stage designs increasingly reach proportions that by far exceed the classical definition of a stage as we know it from theater, musical, or opera productions. Novel stage environments that increasingly require more and effort in terms of architecture, technology, and logistics are being created on a continuous basis. The gigantic open-air touring productions for international stars, for example, can't help but raise the question: "When will we reach the limitations of what can be done within the framework of a concert tour?" But in spite of all the abounding megalomania, an illustrated volume such as this must not lose sight of comparatively smaller productions. At the end of the day, the excellence of the production itself determines what content reaches the spectator on an emotional level. Large-scale productions carry the inherent danger that the audience might lose sight of the essentials, i.e., the artists. Stage designs which appear simplistic at first are quite capable–together with the right production–of touching the spectator just as deeply.

While working on STAGE DESIGN I was frequently surprised by such extraordinary ideas as "ERAR-ITJARITJAKA", in which an important part of the stage design was placed out of the audience's sight behind a white façade. Most of the time the action is actually projected onto the façade by means of cameras and a video projector, by means of which the show becomes accessible to the audience. Or we might take the cross medial

performance "delusions," which plays with the limits of perception. The performers interact with their independent images of self by means of software art. Projections and illusions compose the ever changing stage.

LED surfaces of all shapes and sizes that show videos, pictures or graphic animations are taking on an ever greater role in many a stage design. This is especially true of concert tours and television shows, but also applies to special events. Outstanding examples include productions like "Depeche Mode – Touring The Angel," "George Michael – 25LIVE," "U2 – Vertigo," "Red Hot Chili Peppers – Stadium Arcadium," "Robbie Williams – Close Encounters," "Pop Idol," the "Eurovision Song Contests" from 2006 and 2007, and last but not least the opening ceremony of the "Asian Games 2006" with the largest LED-Screen ever constructed.

I noticed a similarly exciting development when it comes to staging special locations which are incorporated into the stage or become part of its backdrop. One example is the skyline of Frankfurt/Main: to welcome the World Cup, the city hosted the three-evening event SKY ARENA, composed of a combination of lighting effects and large-scale slide projections. With its BLUE GOAL production, the city of Hamburg achieved a similarly successful tie-in with the World Cup 2006. Here 175 blue goals were lit in the evenings, sub-

merging the city in blue light and turning Hamburg itself into a stage. The "ARD Olympia Gala 2004" in Athens made full use of the approximately 2500-year-old temple of Zeus as well as the Acropolis as major elements of its backdrop. A further example is the opening ceremony of the main railway station in Berlin for which a light symphony was composed and performed.

STAGE DESIGN documents a great variety of stage productions from the theater, the opera, concert tours, musicals, TV shows, and special events by means of emotionally charged photographs that display a great richness of detail. For most production, a look behind the scenery grants an insight into the impressive and masterly designed stage constructions. The photos of the productions themselves portray the emotional power of the various stage designs. As photographer and author of STAGE DESIGN, I consider it imperative to create pictures which impart information, inspiration and, last but not least, enjoyment. Thus I hope for you, the reader and the viewer of this book, that my pictures provide exactly this experience.

Aktuelle Bühnenbilder erreichen immer häufiger Dimensionen, die die klassische Definition einer Bühne, wie man sie beispielsweise von Theater-, Musical- oder Opernproduktionen kennt, bei Weitem übersteigen. Ständig entstehen neuartige Bühnenwelten, die mit immer größerem Aufwand in Bezug auf Architektur, Technik und Logistik realisiert werden. Betrachtet man beispielsweise die gigantischen Open-Air-Tourneeproduktionen internationaler Stars, fragt man sich nicht selten: „Wann ist die Grenze des im Rahmen einer Konzerttournee Machbaren erreicht?" Doch bei dieser Gigantomanie darf insbesondere in einem solchen Bildband der Blick auf die vergleichsweise kleinen Produktionen nicht verloren gehen. Denn letztendlich entscheidet die hohe Kunst einer Inszenierung darüber, was den Zuschauer am Ende emotional erreicht. Großflächigkeit birgt schließlich auch die Gefahr, dass der Zuschauer den Blick auf das Wesentliche, nämlich die Künstler, verliert. Auf den ersten Blick simpel erscheinende Bühnenbilder können im Zusammenspiel mit der Inszenierung den Zuschauer mindestens ebenso tief berühren.

Bei der Arbeit zu STAGE DESIGN überraschten mich immer wieder außergewöhnliche Ideen, wie zum Beispiel bei „ERARITJARITJAKA": Ein wesentlicher Teil des Bühnenbildes befindet sich für den Zuschauer nicht einsehbar hinter einer weißen Hausfassade. Die meiste Zeit wird das Geschehen mittels Kameras und eines Videoprojektors

auf die Hausfassade projiziert und erst so für den Zuschauer sichtbar. Oder die crossmediale Performance „delusions". Sie spielt mit den Grenzen der Wahrnehmung. Mittels Software-Kunst interagieren die Darsteller mit dem verselbstständigten Abbild des eigenen Ichs. Projektionen und Illusionen bestimmen den changierenden Bühnenraum.

Es fällt zunehmend auf, dass mit Videos, Bildern und grafischen Animationen bespielbare LED-Flächen unterschiedlichster Art eine immer bedeutendere Rolle innerhalb vieler Bühnenbilder einnehmen. Insbesondere gilt das für die Bereiche Concert Touring und TV-Show, aber auch für Special Events. Herausragend sind hier Produktionen wie „Depeche Mode – Touring The Angel", „George Michael – 25LIVE", „U2 – Vertigo", „Red Hot Chili Peppers – Stadium Arcadium", „Robbie Williams – Close Encounters", „Pop Idol", die „Eurovision Song Contests" der Jahre 2006 und 2007 und nicht zuletzt die Eröffnung der „Asian Games 2006" mit dem größten LED-Screen überhaupt zu nennen.

Eine ebenso spannende Entwicklung sehe ich in der Inszenierung von besonderen Orten, die quasi zur Bühne oder zum Teil einer Bühnenkulisse umfunktioniert werden. Als Beispiel ist hier die Skyline von Frankfurt am Main zu nennen. Mittels einer Inszenierung aus Licht und Großdiaprojektion begrüßte Frankfurt an drei Abenden mit dem

Event SKY ARENA die Fußballweltmeisterschaft 2006 in Deutschland. Eine ebenso gelungene Verbindung zur Fußballweltmeisterschaft 2006 stellte die Stadt Hamburg mit der Inszenierung BLUE GOAL her, bei der 175 Blue Goals die Hansestadt bei Dunkelheit in blaues Licht tauchten und sie so zur Lichtbühne verwandelten. Bei der „ARD Olympia Gala 2004" in Athen dienten der zirka 2.500 Jahre alte Tempel des Zeus und die Akropolis als Kulissenelemente. Ein weiteres Beispiel ist die Eröffnung des Berliner Hauptbahnhofs, für die man eigens eine Lichtsinfonie komponierte und aufführte.

STAGE DESIGN dokumentiert mittels detailreicher und emotionsgeladener Fotografien unterschiedlichste Bühnenproduktionen aus den Bereichen Theater, Oper, Concert Touring, Musical, TV-Show und Special Event. Der Blick hinter die Kulissen gewährt beim überwiegenden Teil der Produktionen Einsicht in die beeindruckenden und meisterlich gestalteten Bühnenkonstruktionen. Die Fotografien der Inszenierungen selbst vermitteln die emotionale Kraft der verschiedenen Bühnenbilder. Mir als Fotograf und Autor von STAGE DESIGN ist es wichtig, Bilder als Informations-, Inspirations- und schließlich als Genussquelle zu schaffen. Somit wünsche ich Ihnen als Leser und Betrachter, dass Ihnen meine Fotografien genau das vermitteln.

Cada vez con más frecuencia, las escenografías actuales alcanzan dimensiones que superan ampliamente la definición clásica de lo que se conoce por un escenario por ejemplo, de producciones teatrales, musicales u operísticas. Continuamente surgen novedosos universos escénicos que se realizan con un despliegue cada vez mayor de arquitectura, técnica y logística. Si uno observa por ejemplo las gigantescas producciones de las giras al aire libre de las estrellas internacionales, es frecuente preguntarse: «¿Cuándo se llega el límite de lo factible en el marco de una gira de conciertos?» Pero entre toda esta gigantomanía no se debe perder de vista producciones comparativamente más pequeñas, especialmente en un libro como éste. Pues a fin de cuentas lo que determina el valor artístico de una puesta en escena es su capacidad para llegar emocionalmente hasta el espectador. Las grandes superficies esconden también el peligro de que el espectador pierda de vista lo más importante, es decir al artista. Escenografías aparentemente sencillas pueden, interactuando con la puesta en escena, conmover al espectador cuando menos con la misma intensidad.

Mientras trabajaba en STAGE DESIGN me sorprendieron una y otra vez ideas extraordinarias, como por ejemplo, en «ERARITJARITJAKA», en la que una parte fundamental de la escenografía se encuentra detrás de la blanca fachada de una casa, fuera del campo visual del espectador. La mayor parte del tiempo, se proyecta el acontecer sobre la fachada de la casa mediante cámaras y un proyector de vídeo, y sólo así resulta visible para el espectador. O la performance intermedial «delusions», la cual juega con los límites de la percepción. Mediante arte software, los actores interactúan con la imagen independizada del propio yo. Proyecciones e ilusiones determinan el espacio escénico cambiante.

Cada vez llama más la atención el hecho de que superficies LED, que se pueden impresionar con vídeos, imágenes y animaciones gráficas, desempeñen un papel cada vez mayor dentro de muchas escenografías, especialmente en el sector de las giras de conciertos y los espectáculos televisivos, pero también para eventos especiales. Aquí destacan producciones como «Depeche Mode – Touring The Angel», «George Michael – 25LIVE», «U2 – Vertigo», «Red Hot Chili Peppers – Stadium Arcadium», «Robbie Williams – Close Encounters», «Pop Idol», las ediciones del «Festival de la Canción de Eurovisión» de los años 2006 y 2007, y por supuesto, no se puede dejar de mencionar la inauguración de los «Asian Games 2006» con las mayores pantallas LED.

Un desarrollo igual de interesante observo en la puesta en escena de lugares especiales que prácticamente se transforman en escenario o en parte de un decorado escénico. Como ejemplo de ello se puede citar el perfil arquitectónico de Fráncfort del Meno. Mediante una puesta en escena a base de luz y de proyecciones de diapositivas de gran formato, la ciudad conmemoró durante tres noches el Campeonato Mundial de Fútbol 2006 en Alemania con el evento SKY ARENA. Igual de bien conseguido estuvo el enlace que la ciudad de Hamburgo estableció con el Mundial de Fútbol 2006 mediante la puesta en escena BLUE GOAL. En la oscuridad, 175 porterías azules sumergían la ciudad hanseática en una luz azul y se convertían así en escenarios lumínicos. Durante la «ARD Olimpia Gala 2004» (gala olímpica del primer canal televisivo alemán) en Atenas, el templo de Zeus de casi 2500 años de antigüedad y la Acrópolis sirvieron como elementos escénicos. Otro ejemplo lo constituye la inauguración de la Estación Central de Berlín, para la que se compuso y dirigió ex profeso una sinfonía lumínica.

Con fotografías detalladas y cargadas de emoción, STAGE DESIGN documenta producciones escénicas procedentes del ámbito del teatro, la ópera, giras de conciertos, musicales, espectáculos televisivos y eventos especiales. La mirada entre bastidores en la mayor parte de las producciones nos permite captar las construcciones escénicas impresionantes y magistralmente realizadas. Las fotografías de las puestas en escena transmiten de por sí la fuerza emocional de las diferentes escenografías. Como fotógrafo y autor de STAGE DESIGN me resulta importante crear imágenes que sean fuente de información, inspiración y finalmente, de placer. Eso es exactamente lo que deseo que mis fotografías le transmitan como lector y observador.

Les scénographies et décors actuels atteignent de plus en plus fréquemment des dimensions qui dépassent de loin la définition classique de la scène telle qu'on la connaît du théâtre, des comédies musicales ou des opéras. On voit constamment apparaître des univers scéniques inédits, réalisés avec des moyens architecturaux, techniques et logistiques toujours plus imposants. À voir, par exemple, les moyens gigantesques mis en oeuvre lors de tournées de concerts open-air de stars internationales, on se demande souvent quand seront atteintes les limites du possible en la matière. Mais tout ce gigantisme ne doit pas faire oublier non plus les autres productions comparativement plus modestes, a fortiori dans le cadre d'un tel ouvrage. Car c'est en effet la maîtrise de la mise en scène qui détermine en dernière instance ce qui va ou non toucher le spectateur. À trop vouloir étendre la surface des écrans ou de la scène, on risque fort de faire perdre de vue l'essentiel au spectateur, à savoir les artistes. Si la mise en scène suit, des décors en apparence dépouillés peuvent émouvoir tout aussi profondément le spectateur, sinon plus.

Durant les travaux préparatoires à STAGE DESIGN, j'ai été plus d'une fois saisi par l'originalité de certaines idées. Ainsi, dans le cas d'« ERARITJARITJAKA », spectacle musical durant lequel une part essentielle du décor, masquée par la façade blanche d'une maison, reste inaccessible au spectateur qui, la plupart du temps, ne peut voir l'action que grâce à des projections sur cette façade, par le truchement de caméras et d'un projecteur vidéo. Pour « Delusions », performance crossmédia jouant avec les limites de la perception, les interprètes interagissent avec le reflet autonomisé de leur propre Moi, grâce à l'art numérique. Ici, ce sont des projections et des illusions qui délimitent et définissent un espace scénique changeant.

De plus en plus, on remarque la place grandissante que prennent dans de nombreuses scénographies les écrans LED, de types les plus divers et reproduisant aussi bien des vidéos que des images ou des animations graphiques. Cela vaut en particulier pour les tournées de concerts ou les retransmissions télévisées, mais aussi pour les événements spéciaux. On se souvient notamment de certaines tournées, comme celles de Depeche Mode (« Touring the Angel »), de George Michael (« 25LIVE »), de U2 (« Vertigo »), des Red Hot Chili Peppers (« Stadium Arcadium »), de Robbie Williams (« Close Encounters »), de l'émission britannique « Pop Idol », mais aussi des éditions 2006 et 2007 du Concours Eurovision de la Chanson, sans oublier l'ouverture des Jeux asiatiques de 2006, et le plus grand écran LED jamais construit à ce jour.

Je vois dans la mise en scène de lieux particuliers, transformés tantôt intégralement en scène, tantôt en partie de mur de scène, une autre évolution tout aussi intéressante. Je pense par exemple à la Skyline de Francfort-sur-le-Main : à l'occasion de la Coupe du monde de football 2006 en Allemagne, la ville a organisé trois soirées durant le « SKY ARENA », un son et lumière accompagné de projections de diapo-

sitives géantes. Toujours en rapport avec la Coupe du monde de football 2006 et tout aussi réussi, le « BLUE GOAL » mis en scène par la ville de Hambourg, durant lequel 175 Blue Goals nocturnes plongèrent l'ancienne cité hanséatique dans de la lumière bleue, la transformant ainsi en scène lumineuse. Pour l'« ARD Olympia Gala 2004 » à Athènes (gala d'ouverture des Jeux olympiques d'Athènes de 2004 organisé par la chaîne allemande ARD), ce furent le temple de Zeus, vieux de quelque 2 500 ans, et l'Acropole elle-même qui servirent d'éléments de décor. Autre exemple encore : l'inauguration de la nouvelle gare centrale de Berlin, qu'accompagna une véritable symphonie de lumières, composée spécialement pour cette occasion.

Par ses photographies riches de détails et chargées d'émotion, STAGE DESIGN constitue une sorte de documentaire sur des productions scéniques les plus diverses, issues du théâtre, de l'opéra, de tournées de concerts, de comédies musicales, de shows télévisés et d'événements spéciaux. Pour la plupart d'entre elles, ces coups d'œil jetés en coulisse permettent de découvrir des structures et architectures scéniques impressionnantes de maîtrise, tandis que les photographies de la mise en scène elle-même restituent la puissance émotionnelle générée par les différents décors. Pour le photographe et auteur de STAGE DESIGN que je suis, il est important que les images soient à la fois source d'information et d'inspiration, mais aussi de plaisir. C'est tout ce que je vous souhaite à vous, lecteur et observateur, de retrouver en parcourant mes photographies.

Il panorama attuale della scenografia raggiunge sempre più spesso dimensioni tali da superare i confini del concetto di palcoscenico tipico delle produzioni teatrali, operistiche o di musical. Nascono scenografie sempre nuove, realizzate con grande dispendio di mezzi tecnici, architettonici e logistici. Quando si pensa, per esempio, alle mastodontiche produzioni per i concerti open-air in occasione delle tourneé di star internazionali, viene spontaneo chiedersi se ormai non sia stato raggiunto il limite estremo. Ma pur nella corsa verso il gigantesco, in un volume illustrato come questo è importante non trascurare le produzioni più piccole. In ultima analisi, infatti, è l'arte della scenografia a determinare ciò che tocca le corde emozionali dello spettatore. La mera grandezza delle dimensioni corre il rischio di far deviare lo sguardo dello spettatore dall'elemento fondamentale, l'artista. Scenografie apparentemente semplici, invece, possono interagire con la messa in scena per ottenere lo stesso livello di coinvolgimento emotivo dello spettatore.

Durante il lavoro per la realizzazione di STAGE DESIGN sono stato colpito più volte da idee nuove e originali, come nel caso di "ERARITJARITJAKA", in cui la scenografia si trova quasi interamente dietro la facciata bianca di una casa, invisibile allo spettatore; la rappresentazione viene in gran parte proiettata sulla facciata dell'edificio attraverso cineprese e un videoproiettore e così diventa visibile al pubblico. Un altro esempio è la performance multimediale "delusions", che gioca con i confini della percezione e in cui gli attori interagiscono con l'immagine autonoma del proprio Io per mezzo di arte-software. Le proiezioni e le illusioni scandiscono uno spazio della rappresentazione in continuo mutamento.

Nel panorama della scenografia oggi giocano un ruolo sempre più importante le superfici a LED delle più svariate tipologie, utilizzate per video, immagini e animazioni grafiche, soprattutto nelle tournée e negli spettacoli televisivi, ma anche per eventi speciali. Possiamo citare produzioni di eccezionale livello come "Depeche Mode – Touring The Angel", "George Michael – 25LIVE", "U2 – Vertigo", "Red Hot Chili Peppers – Stadium Arcadium", "Robbie Williams – Close Encounters", "Pop Idol", gli "Eurovision Song Contests" del 2006 e del 2007 e non ultima la cerimonia di apertura degli "Asian Games 2006", con il più grande schermo a LED mai visto prima.

Una tendenza altrettanto interessante è a mio parere l'allestimento di particolari luoghi che divengono essi stessi palcoscenico o parte dell'impianto scenografico, come la skyline di Francoforte sul Meno, per fare un esempio. Per tre sere, con SKY ARENA, Francoforte ha dato il benvenuto ai Campionati Mondiali di Calcio 2006 attraverso una scenografia di luci e diapositive proiettate in grande formato. Un altro evento degno di nota legato ai Mondiali è stato organizzato dalla città di Amburgo, che ha messo in scena lo spettacolo BLUE GOAL, durante il quale 175 Blue Goal hanno rotto l'oscurità e immerso la città anseatica in una luce blu, per trasformarla in un palcoscenico luminoso. In occasione dell' "ARD Olympia Gala 2004" di Atene il tempio di Zeus e l'Acropoli, con i loro quasi 2.500 anni di storia, sono stati utilizzati come elementi scenografici. Un altro esempio è l'inaugurazione della stazione centrale di Berlino, per la quale è stata composta ed eseguita una sinfonia di luci.

Le fotografie ricche di dettagli ed emozioni di STAGE DESIGN documentano le più diverse produzioni scenografiche in numerosi ambiti: teatro, opera, tournée di concerti, musical, spettacoli televisivi ed eventi speciali. Lo sguardo sui retroscena rivela, nella maggior parte delle produzioni, i segreti delle scenografie di maggior impatto e di più raffinata concezione. Le immagini delle scenografie, a loro volta, trasmettono la forza emotiva delle diverse scenografie. In qualità di fotografo e autore di STAGE DESIGN ritengo fondamentale creare immagini che siano fonte di informazione, ispirazione e piacere, e mi auguro che le mie fotografie riescano a trasmettere al lettore esattamente questo.

THEATER

ERARITJARITJAKA
Conception & Direction: Heiner Goebbels
Scenography and Lighting: Klaus Grünberg
Luxembourg, Luxembourg | 2006

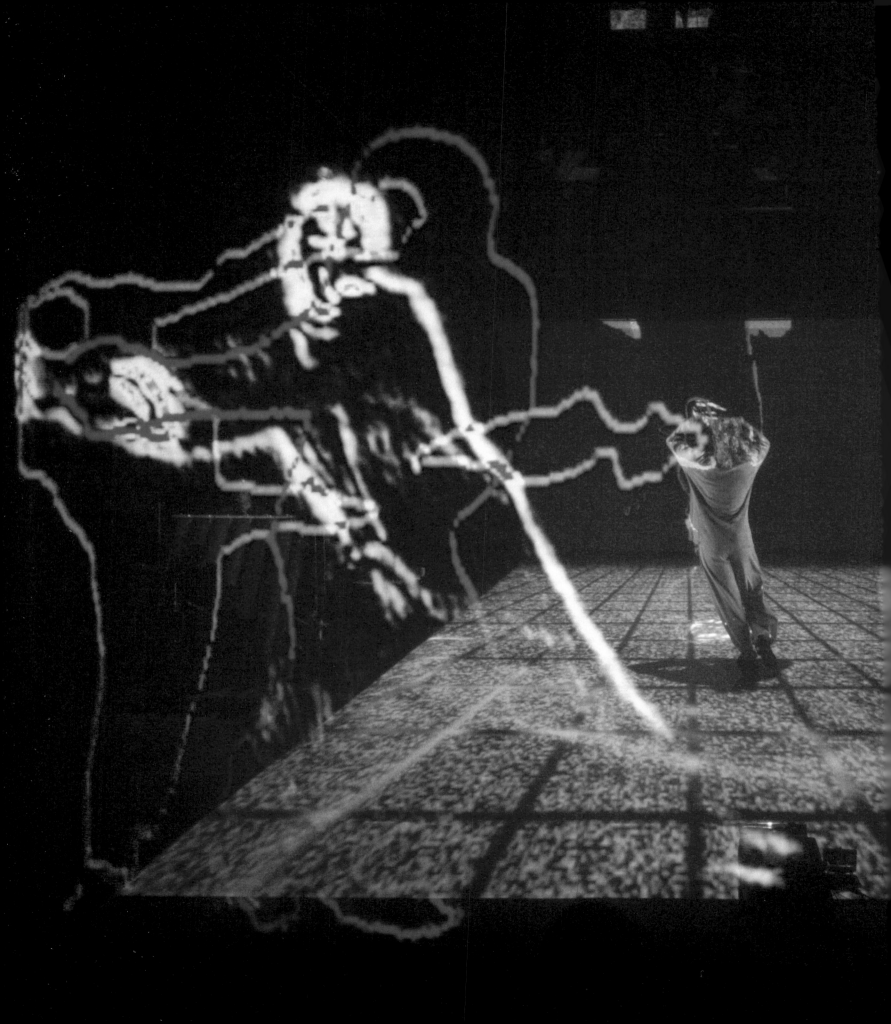

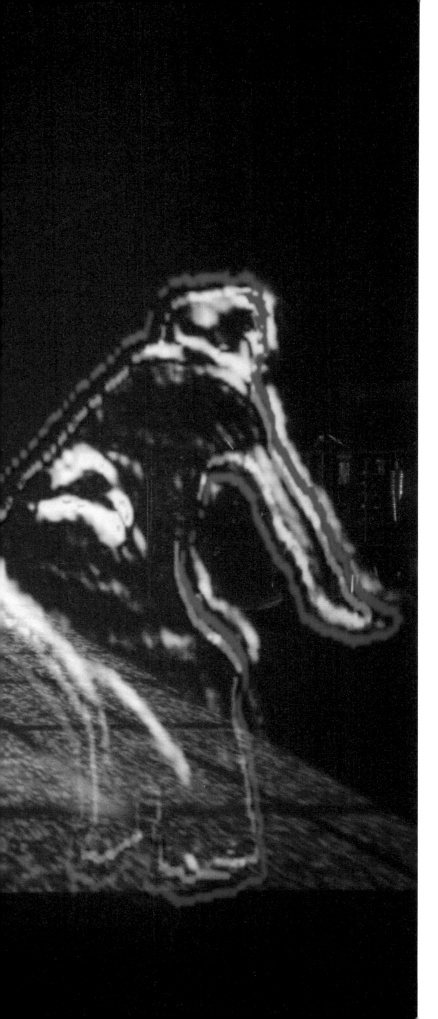

delusions
Production: phase7 performing.arts, Forum
Neues Musiktheater of the Stuttgart State Opera
Art Director: Sven Sören Beyer
Stuttgart, Germany | 2005

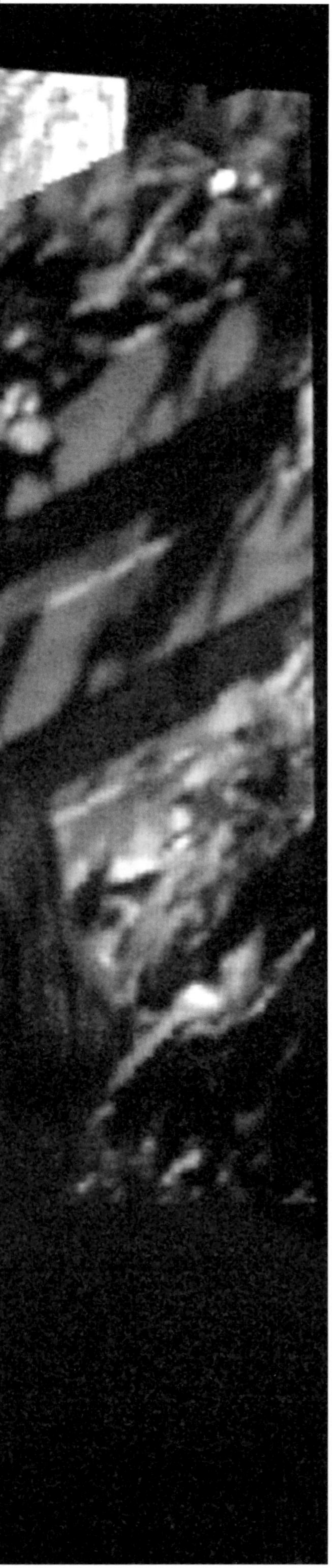

TU DDUI RD IDRE RD.E R .

SIND WIR UNS
WARST DU

DENKST DU
BIN ICH
DU MIR UN
WER WAREN

SIND SIE U
DU ICH, WE
GEDACHT,
BEIDE.

UND ALLE

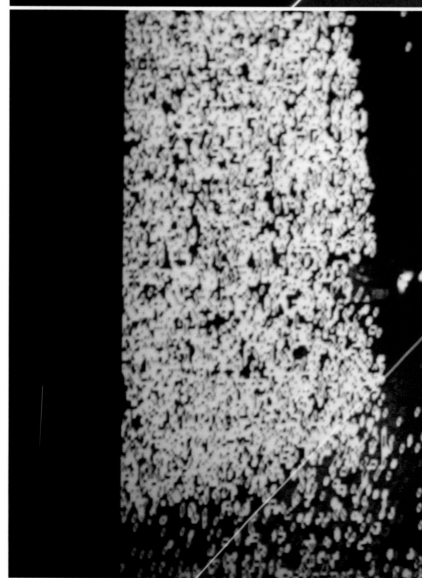

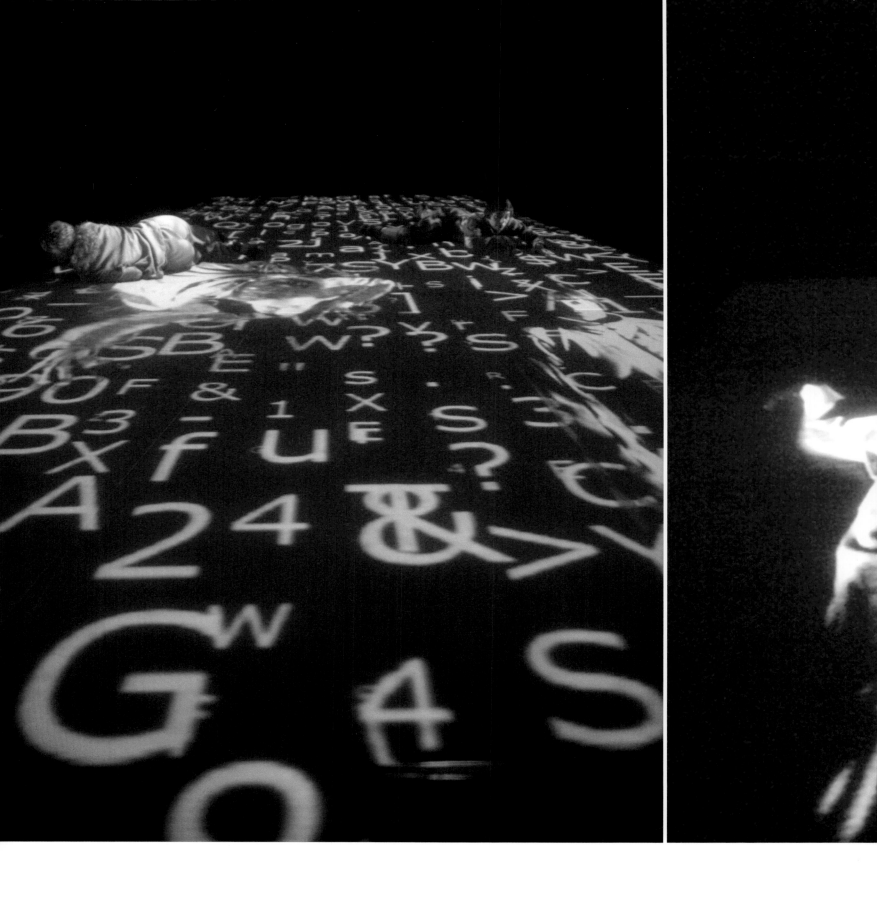

Landscape with distant relatives
Music & Direction: Heiner Goebbels
Scenography and Lighting: Klaus Grünberg
Photographs taken in Amsterdam, Docklands
Netherlands | 06/11/2003 – 06/13/2003

OPERAS

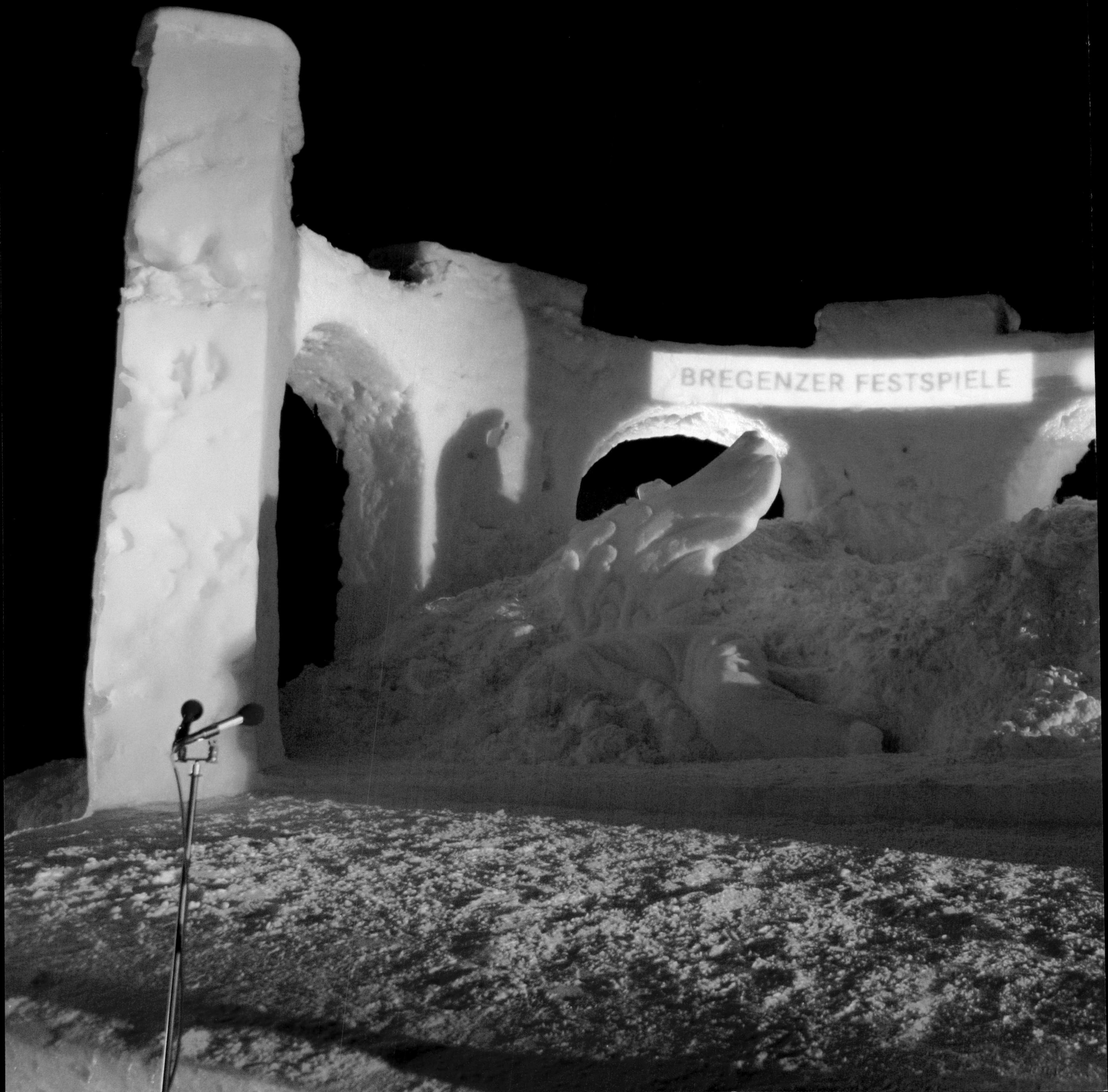
BREGENZER FESTSPIELE

Tosca In The Snow
Director: Dorothée Schaeffer
Lech am Arlberg, Austria | 2007

Turandot
Director: Zhang Yimou
VELTINS-Arena Gelsenkirchen, Germany | 2005

Il Trovatore
Director: Robert Carsen
Water Stage Bregenz, Austria | 2006

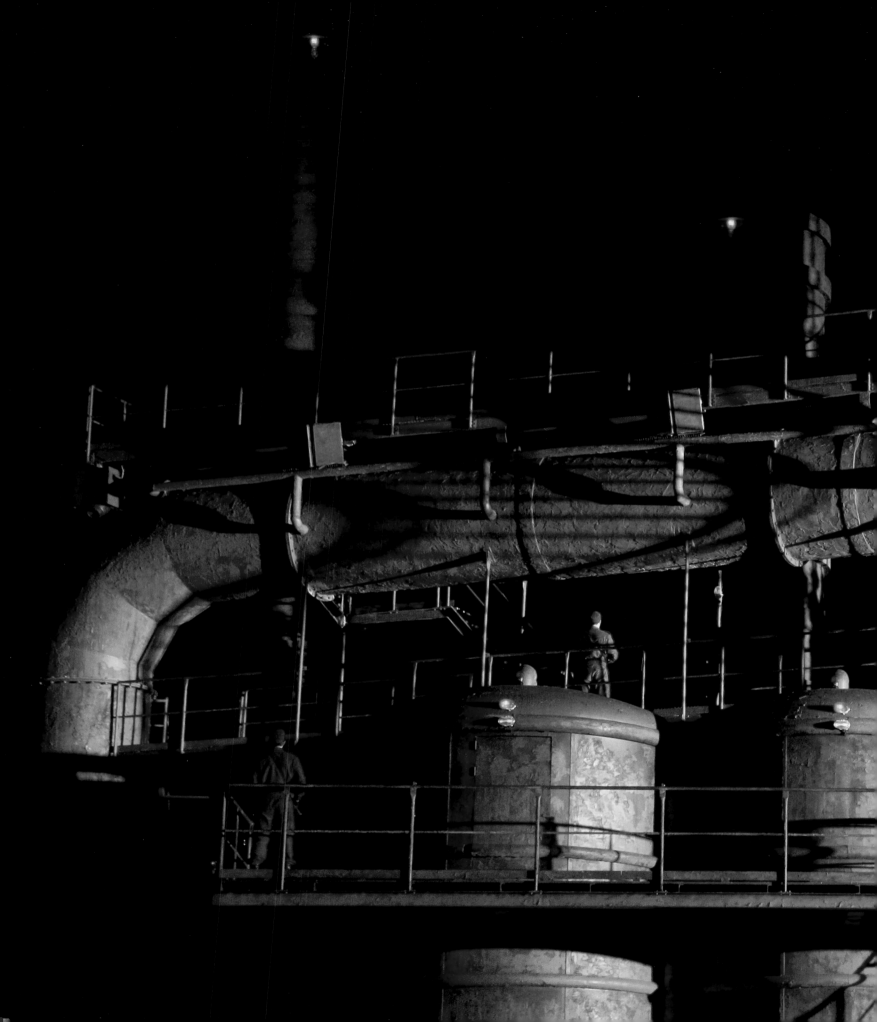

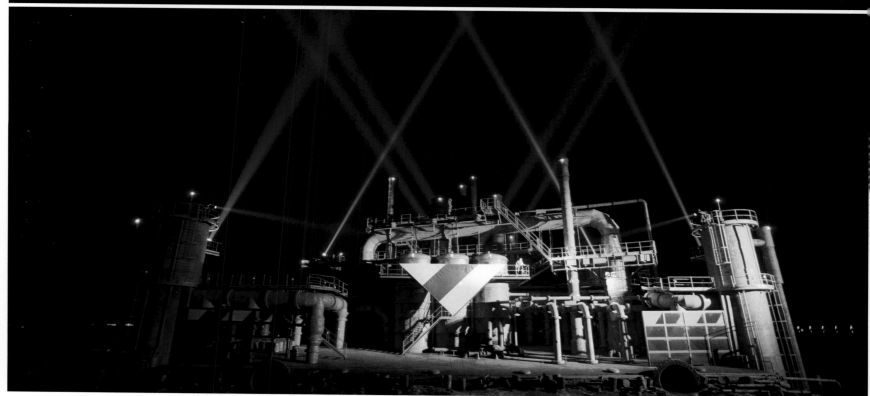

Richard Wagner's The Flying Dutchman
Overall Director: General Manager Guy Montavon
"Domplatz" Erfurt, Germany | 2002

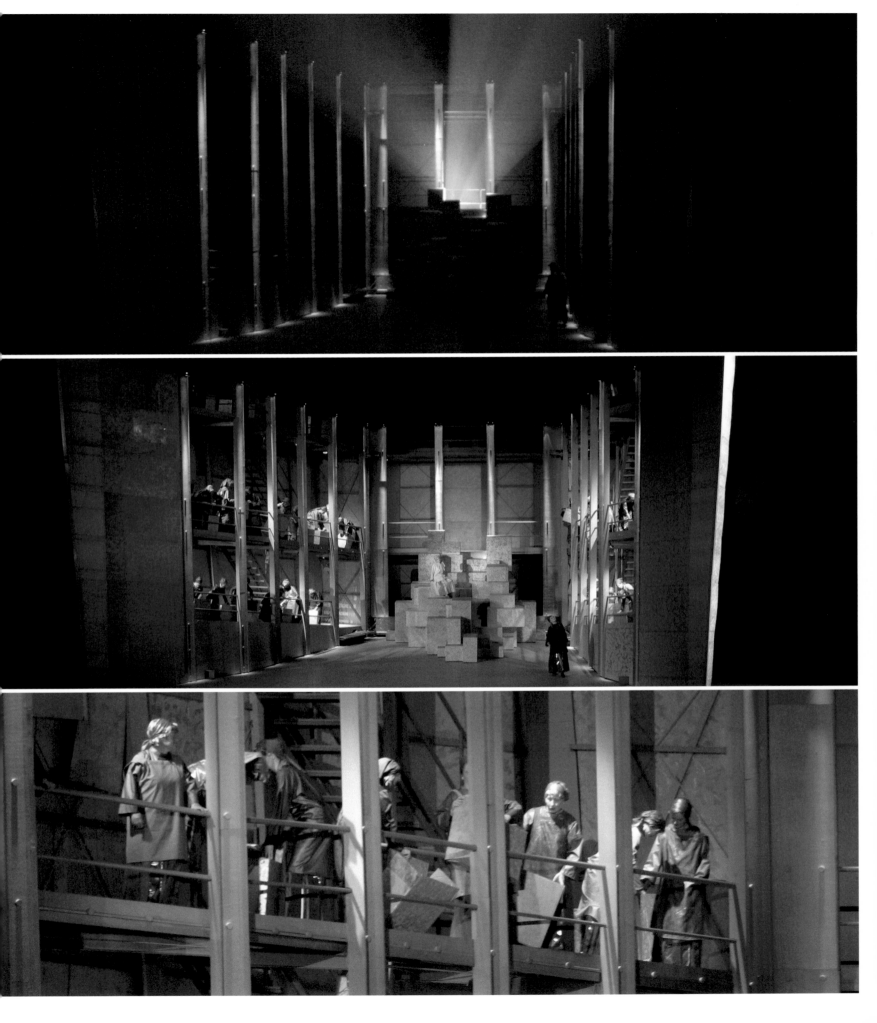

MUSICALS

Disneys DER KÖNIG DER LÖWEN/
Disney's THE LION KING
"Theater im Hafen" Hamburg, Germany | 2007

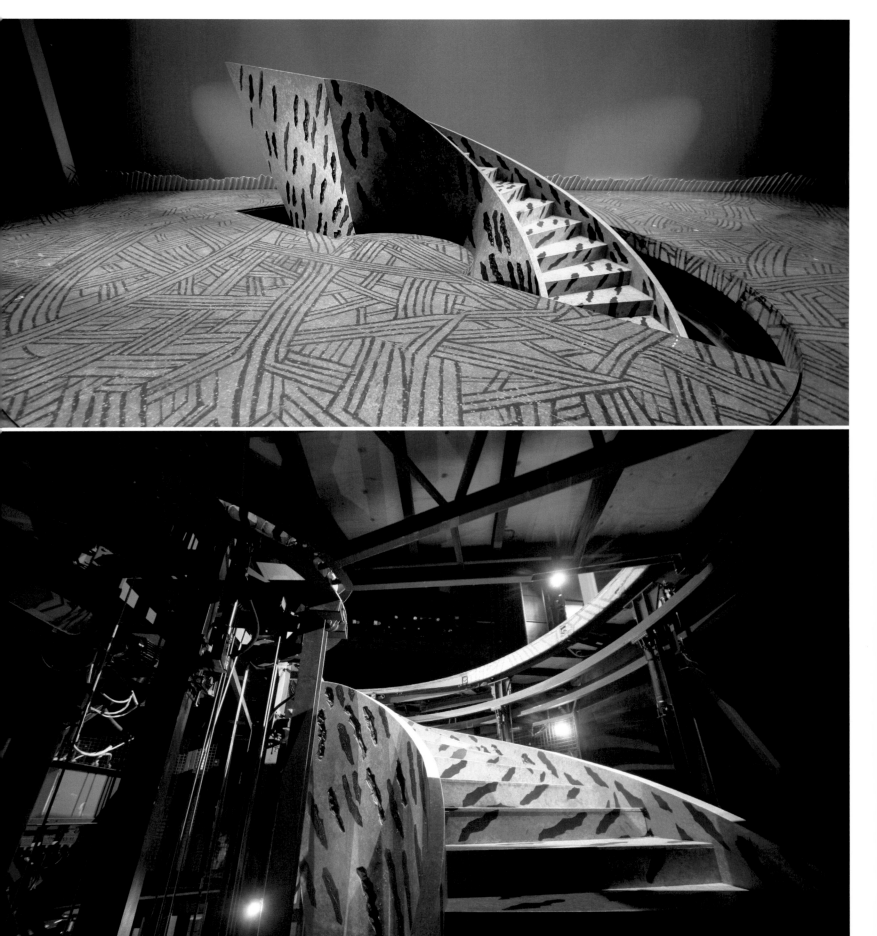

We Will Rock You
Photographs taken in Cologne, Musical Dome
Germany | 2007

130

Starlight Express
Bochum Theater, Germany | 2007

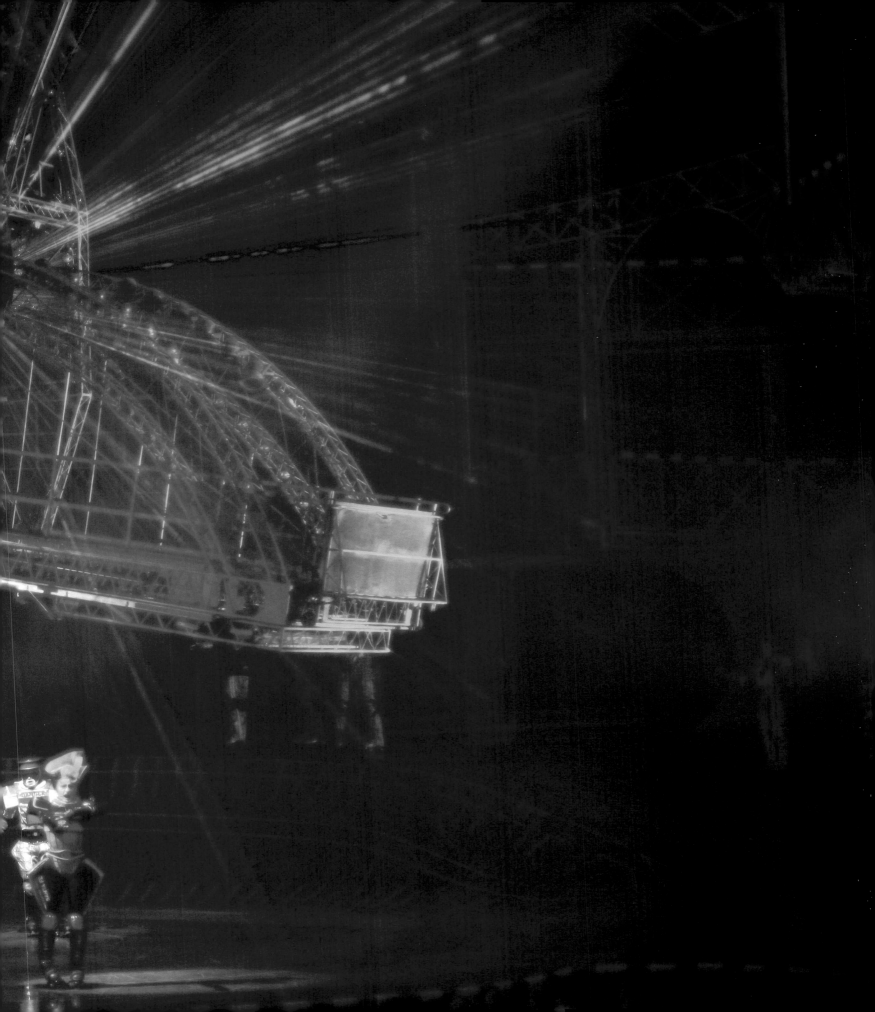

High Fidelity
Colonial Theatre Boston, USA
Imperial Theater NYC, USA | 2006

148

CONCERT TOURINGS

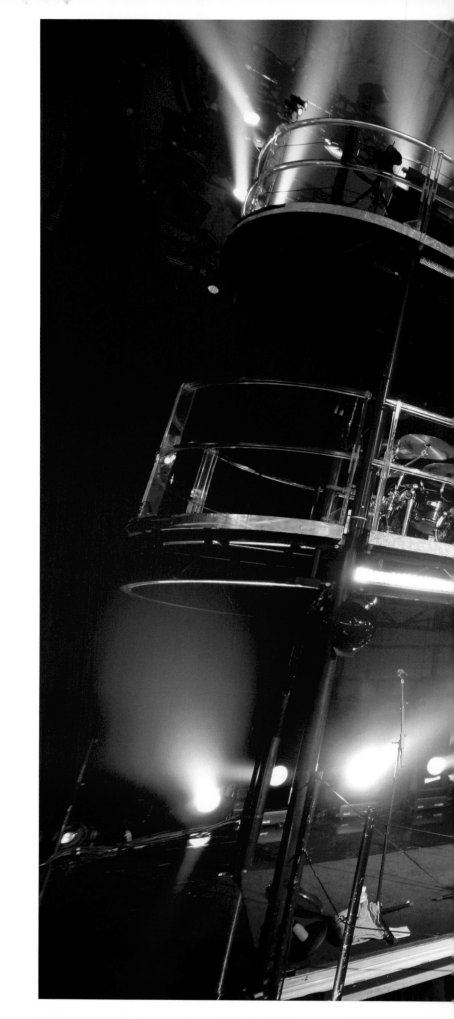

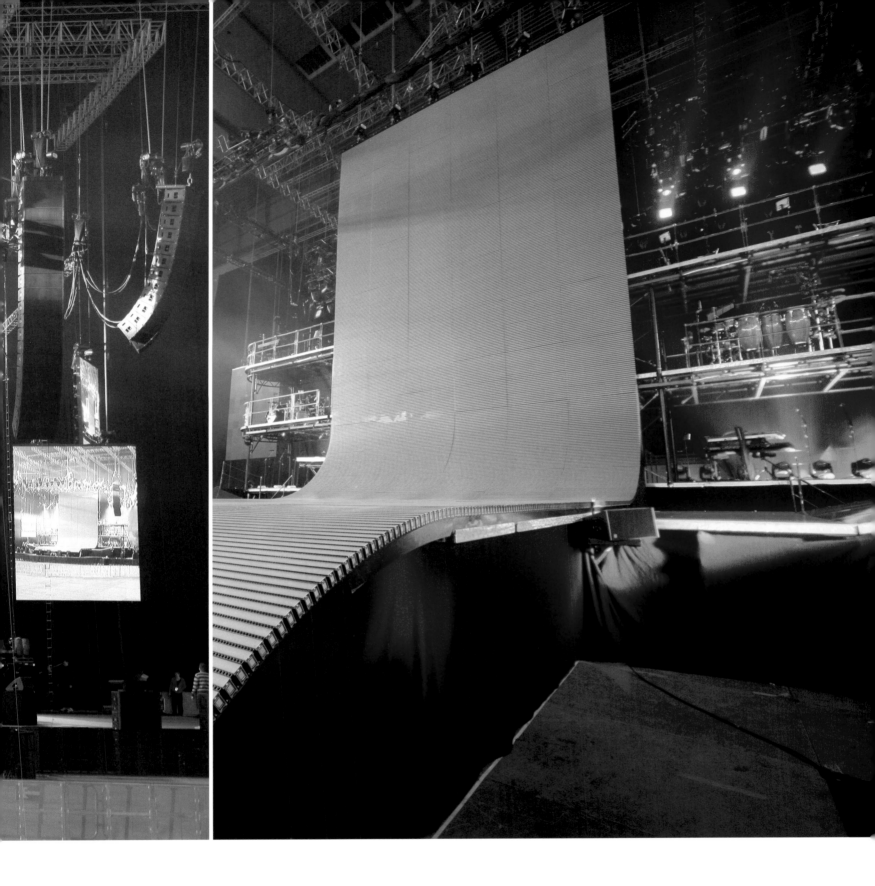

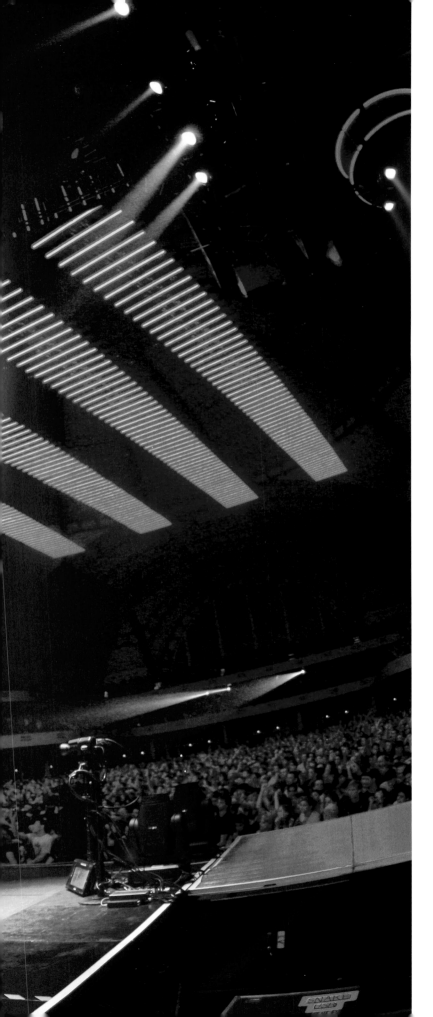

Red Hot Chili Peppers
Stadium Arcadium World Tour
"Festhalle" Frankfurt, Germany | 2006

Bon Jovi
Have A Nice Day
Olympic Stadium Munich, Germany | 2006

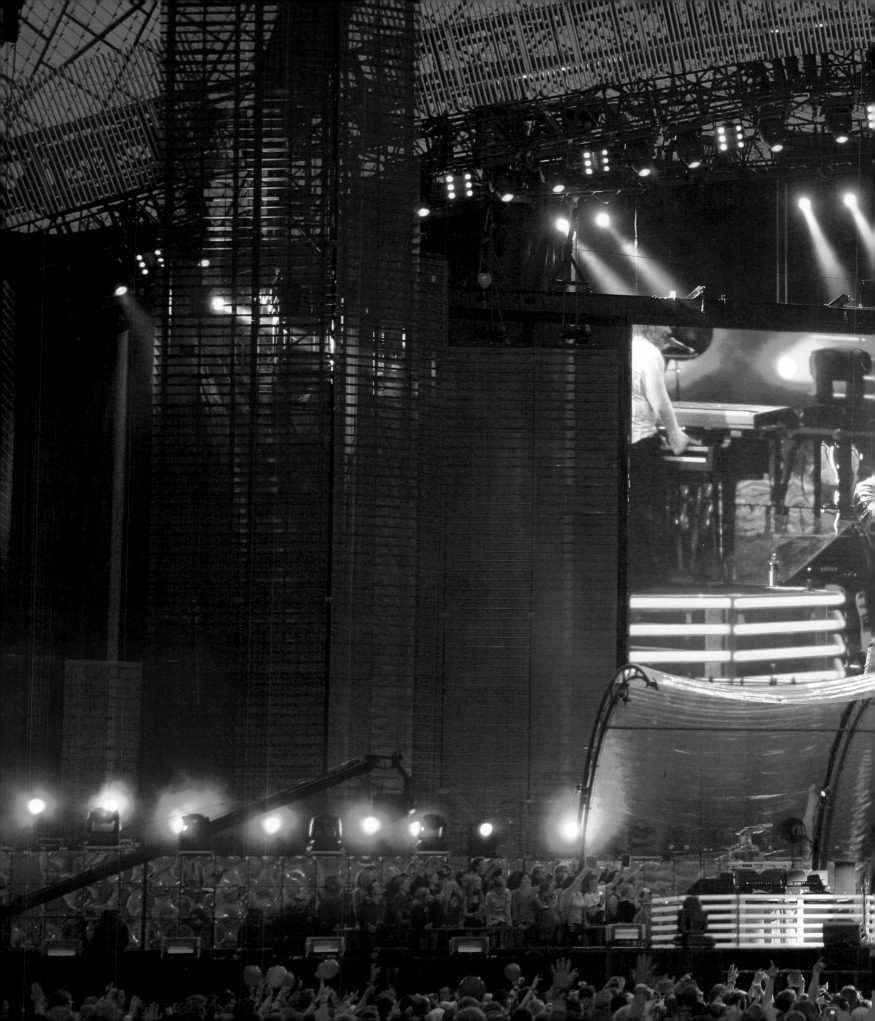

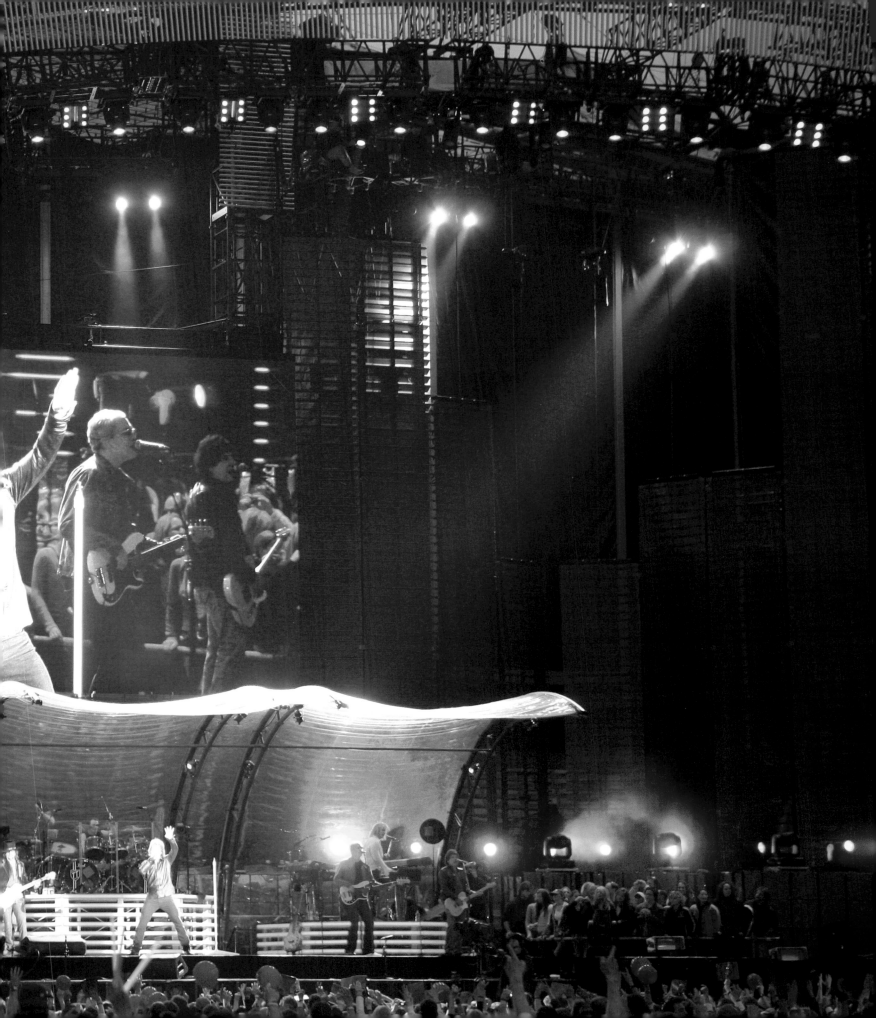

Depeche Mode
Touring The Angel
Olympic Hall Munich, Germany
"Festwiese" Leipzig, Germany | 2006

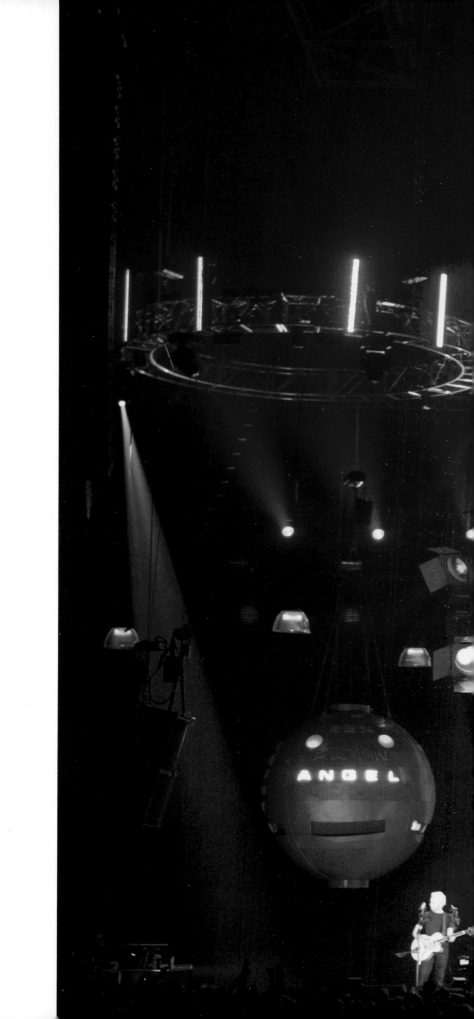

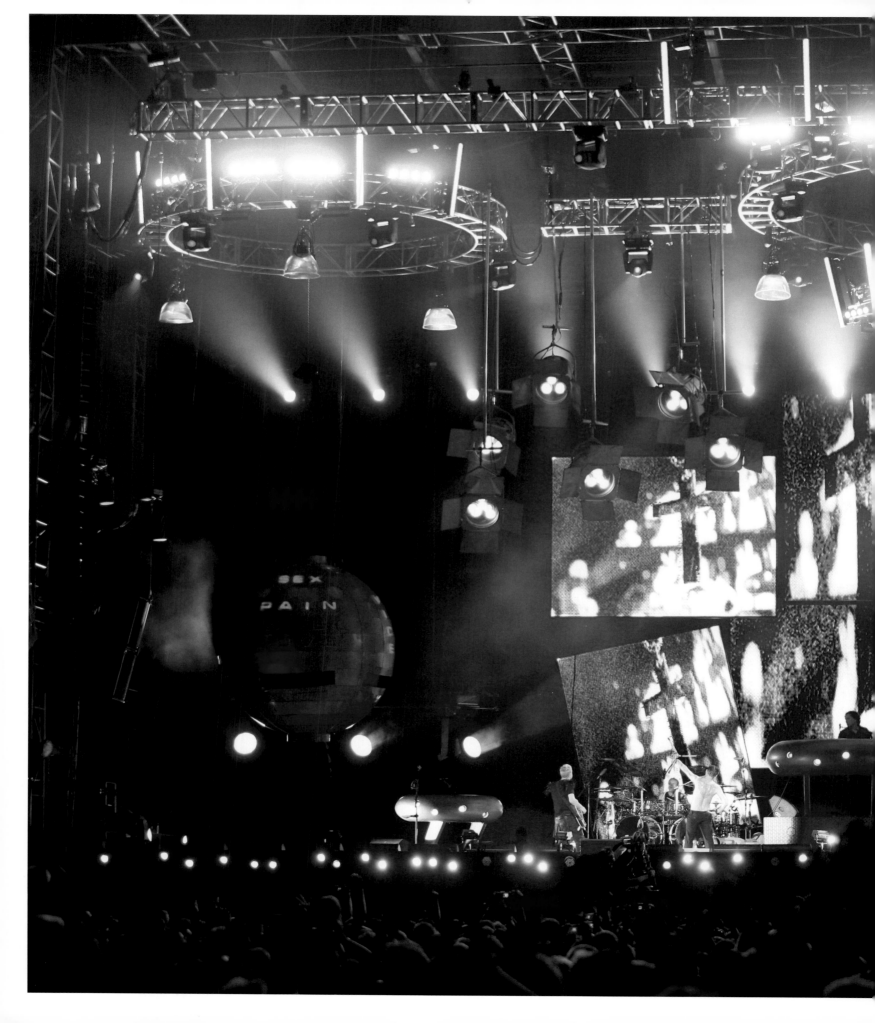

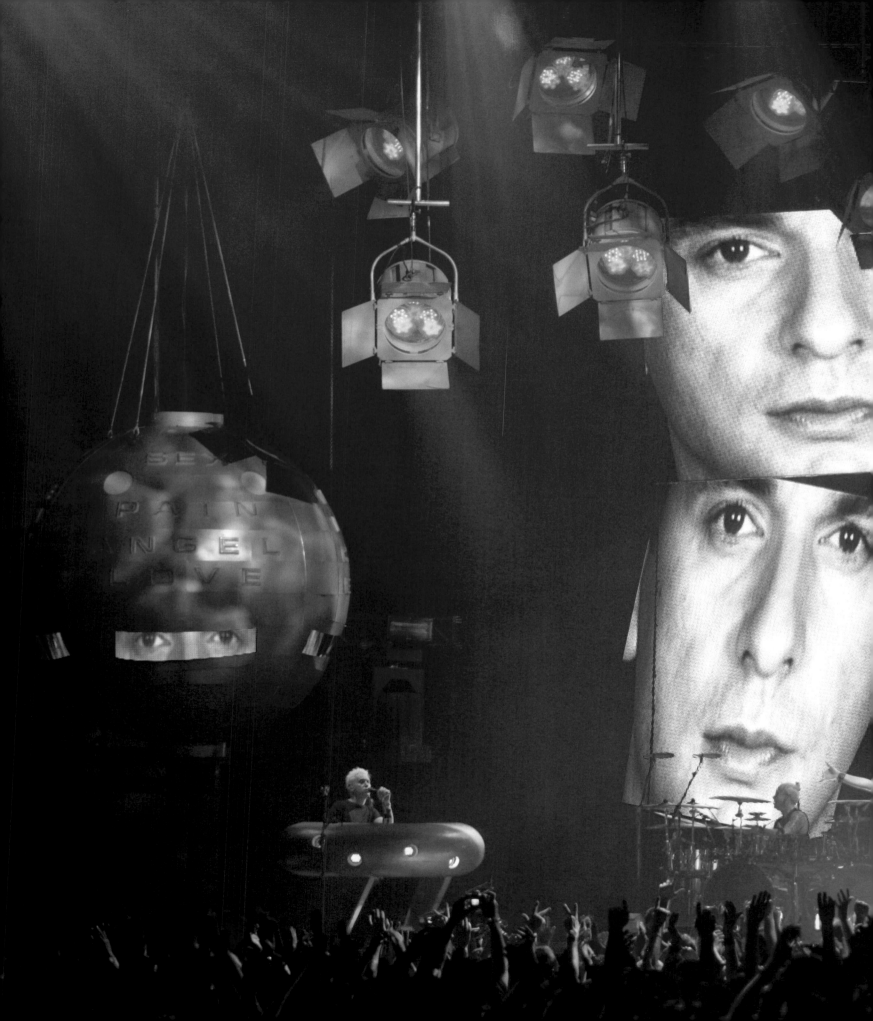

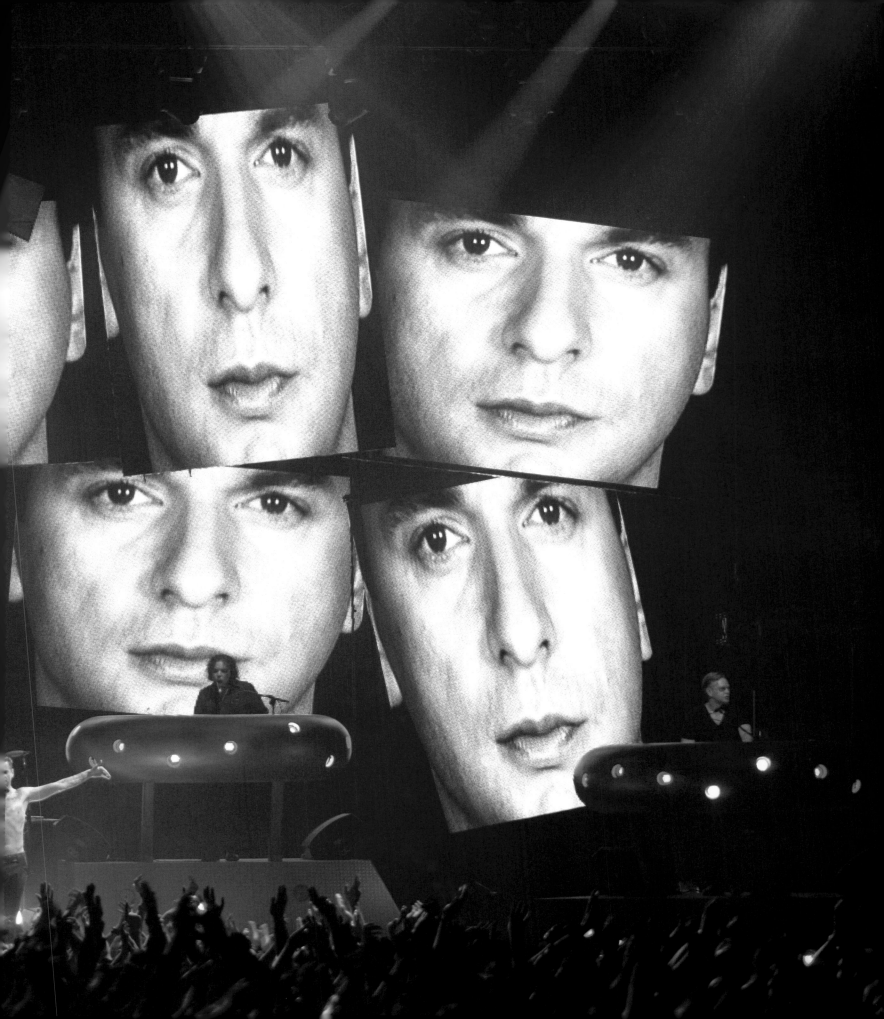

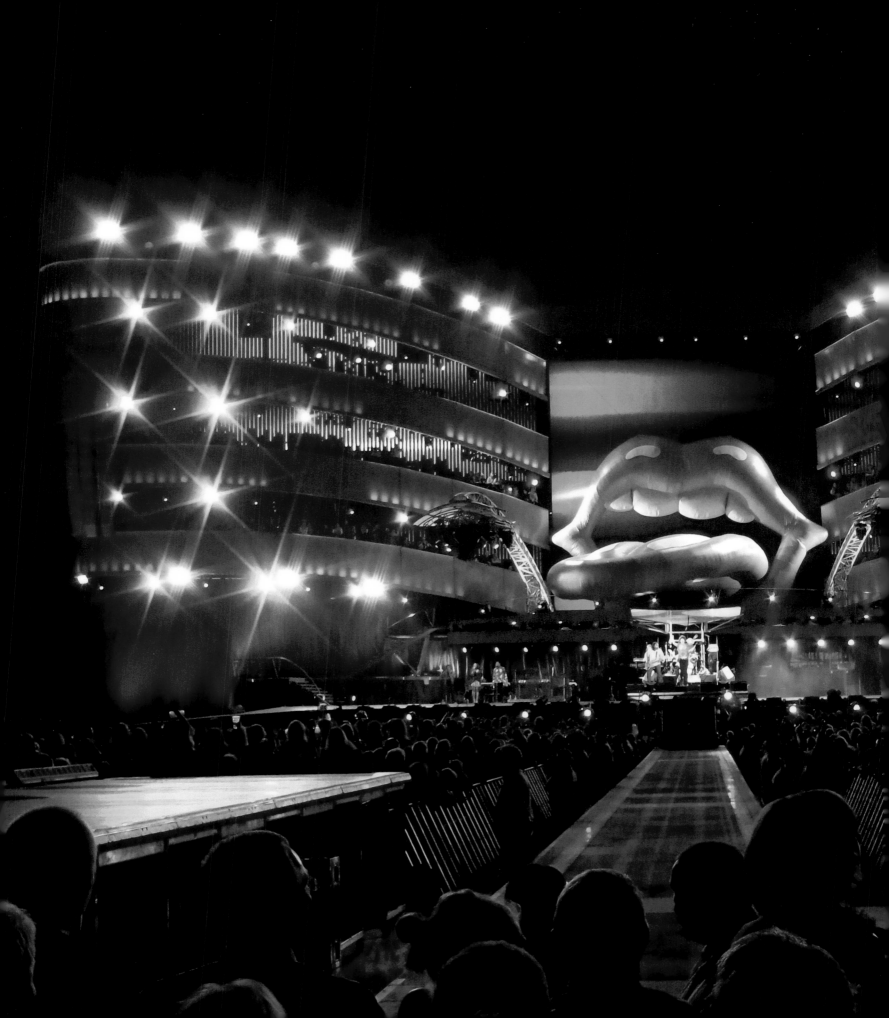

Rolling Stones
A Bigger Bang
Olympic Stadium Berlin, Germany
Twickenham Stadium London, UK | 2005/2006

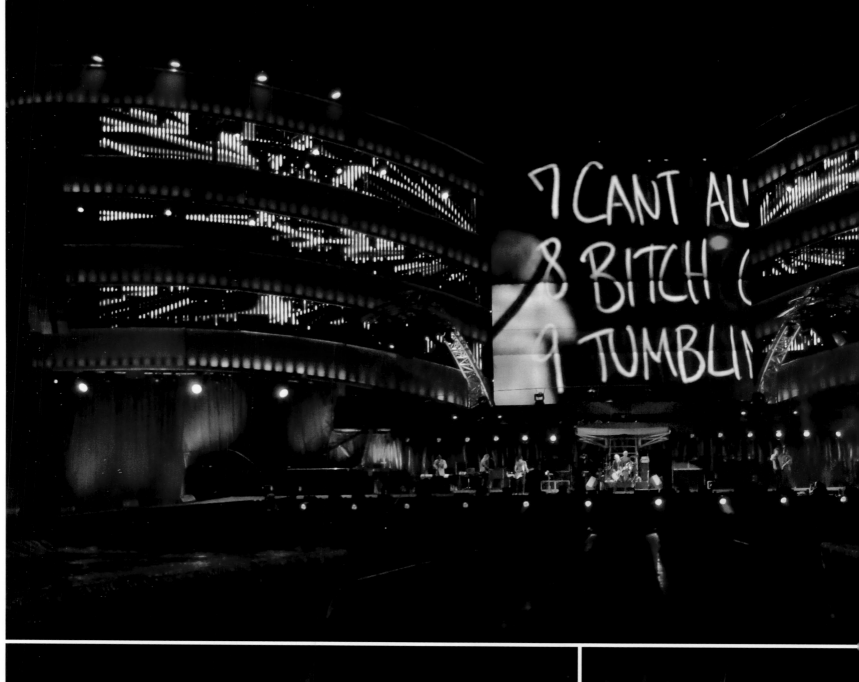

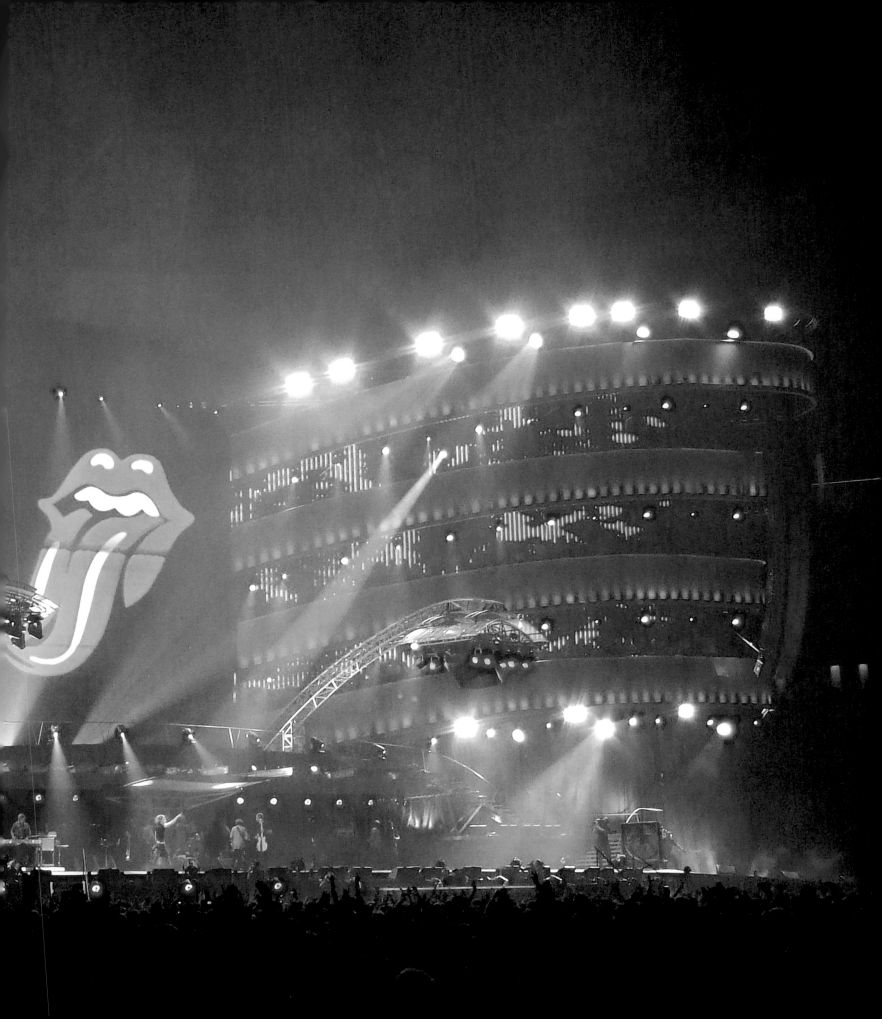

U2
Vertigo
Olympic Stadium Berlin, Germany
VELTINS-Arena Gelsenkirchen, Germany | 2005

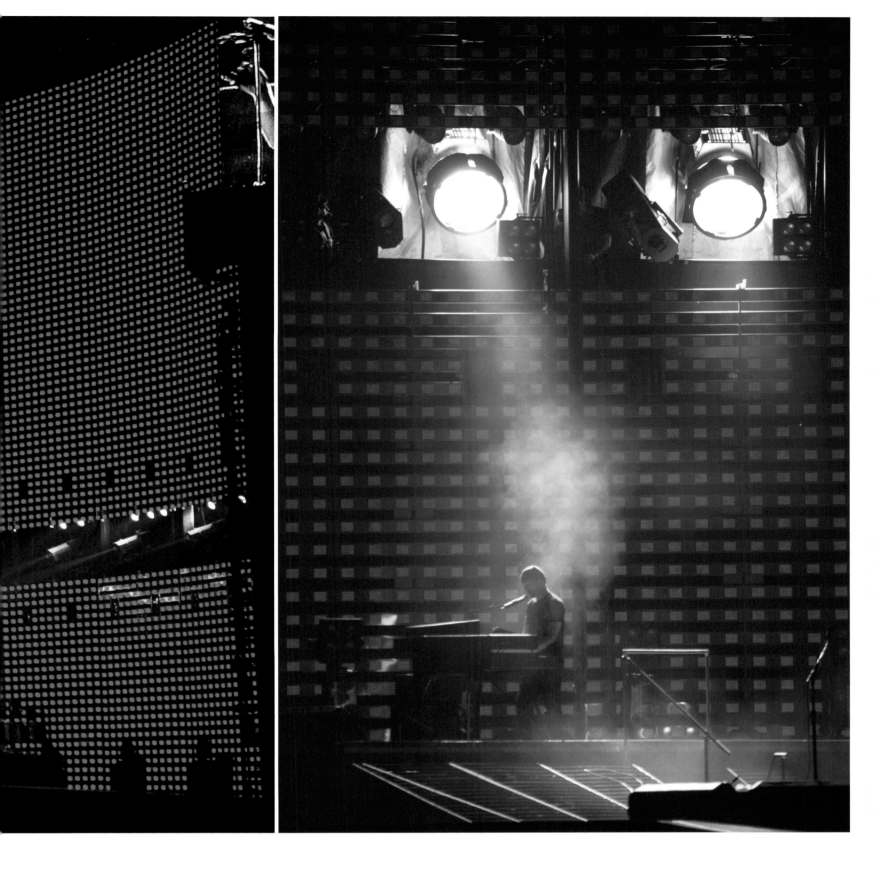

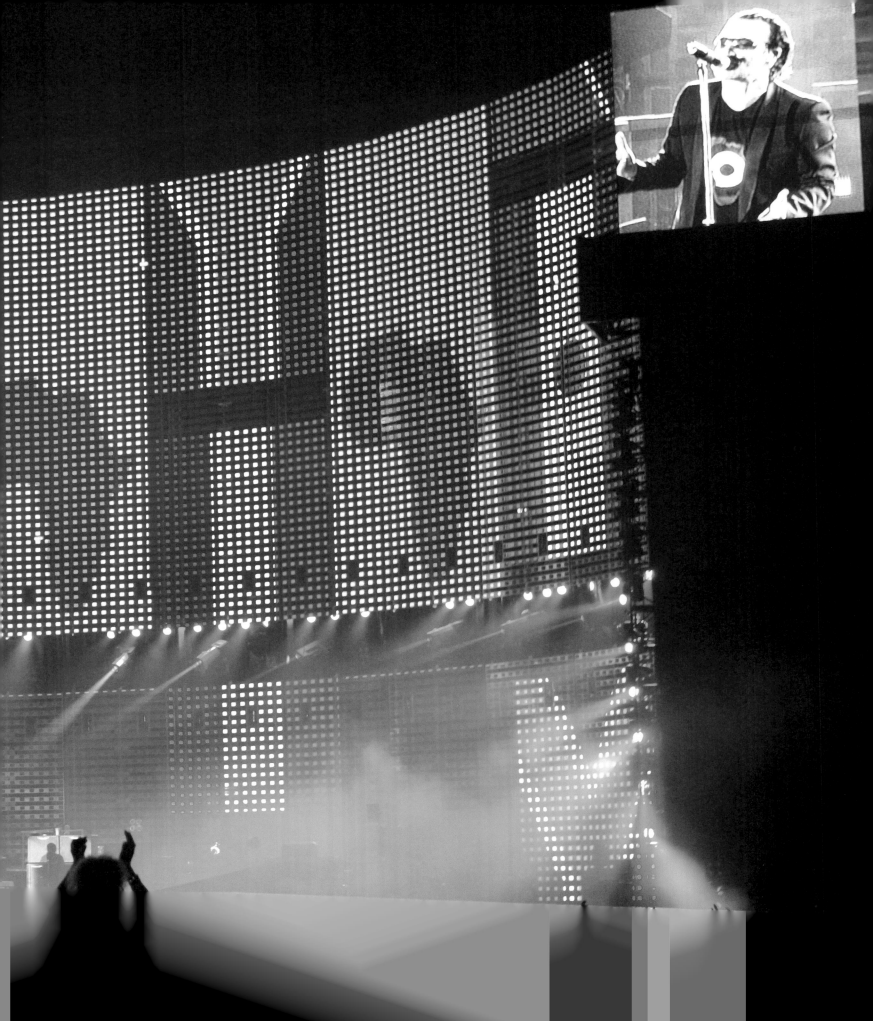

Robbie Williams
Close Encounters
Olympic Stadium Berlin, Germany | 2006

WRIST ACTION

Fig 20

TV-SHOWS

Eurovision Song Contest
Olympic Indoor Arena Athens, Greece | 2006

ARD Olympic Gala
Olympeion Athens, Greece | 2004

Echo
"Palais am Funkturm" at the Berlin Exhibition Grounds
Germany | 2007

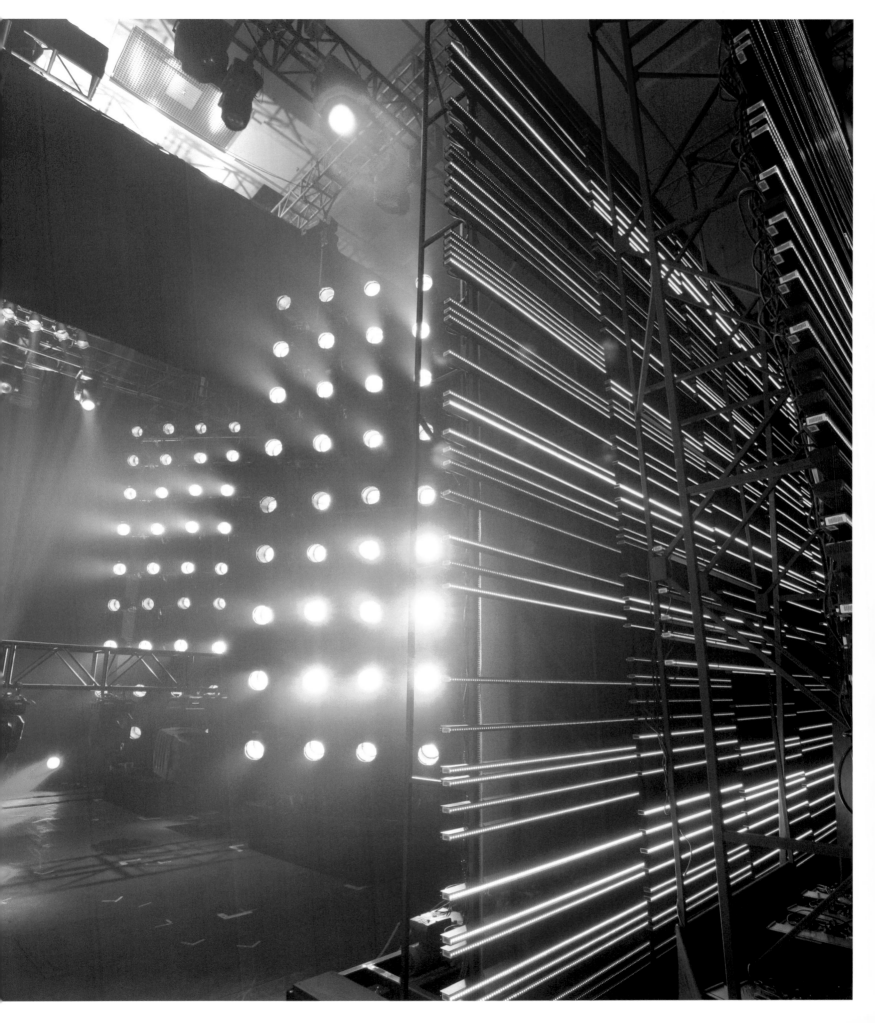

Pop Idol 2006 - Finals
MMC Studios Cologne, Germany | 2006

Eurovision Song Contest
Helsinki, Finland | 2007

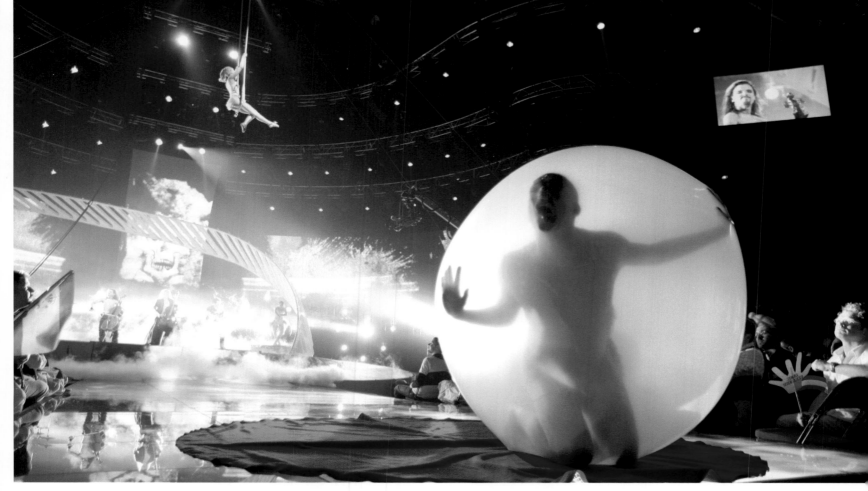

SPECIAL EVENTS

Opening Ceremony of the 15th Asian Games
Doha, Qatar | 2006

SkyArena Frankfurt
Overture to the 2006 FIFA World Cup Germany™
Frankfurt, Germany | 2006

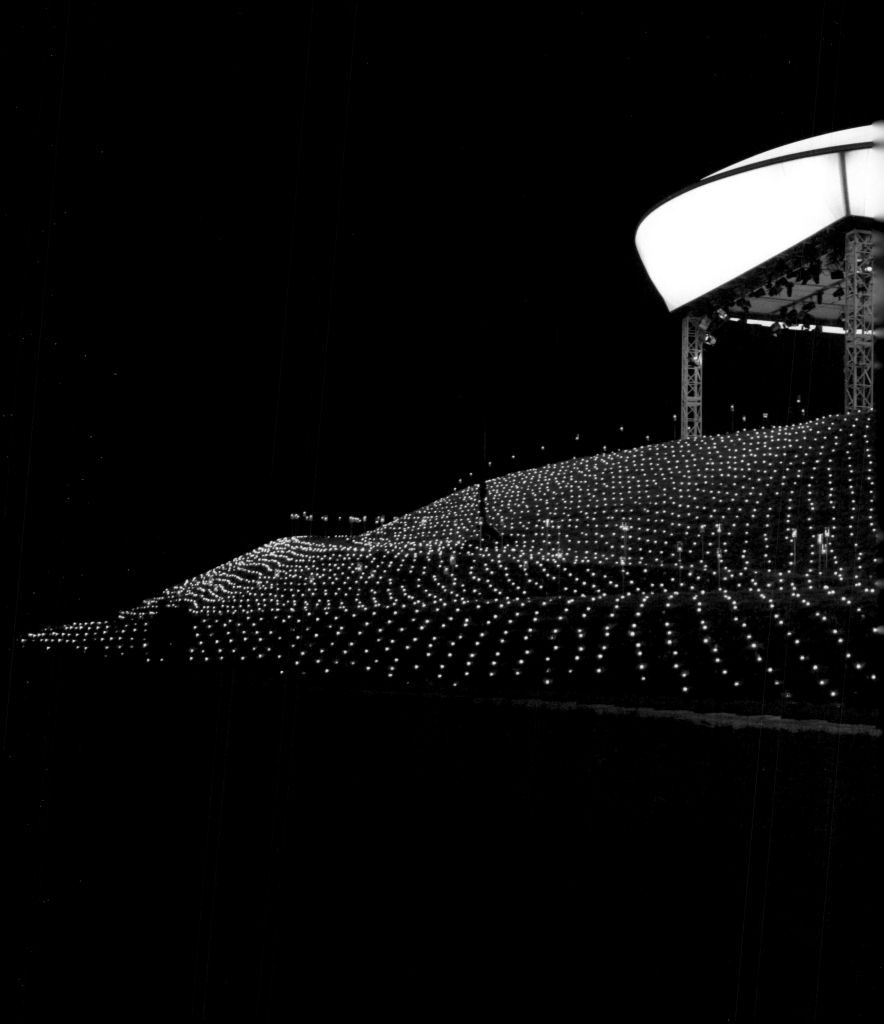

Blue Goals
Hamburg, Germany | 2006

Afrika! Afrika!
Initiator: André Heller
Hamburg City Park, Germany
Cologne-Deutz, Germany | 2006/2007

Symphony Of Light
Berlin's central station, Germany | 2006

BIOGRAPHY

Ralph Larmann initially studied drumming with the main focus on popular music at the Rotterdam Conservatorium. In 1991, however, he decided to change tack and took up an interest in photography and journalism. Since 1992 he has been designing and producing high quality illustrated books, concert brochures, and exhibition catalogues, for artists and companies from the rock, pop, and classical music scenes. In 2000 he founded his own full-service business, the Ralph Larmann Company. Working internationally as a freelance photographer and author, he creates elaborate photo and text documentaries for businesses, artists, lighting designers, and magazines. Since 1989 Ralph Lahrmann has captured countless stars and events in fascinating photographs. The exhibition entitled "Kraft des Augenblicks – Konzert and Eventfotografie" (Power of the Moment – Concert and Event Photography), which was presented in cooperation with Lightpower and staged as part of the music fair 2007 and Prolight+Sound 2007, introduced a selection of his oeuvre in large-scale format (96.5 x 70 in.) and was presented in the Galleria on the premises of the Frankfurt trade fair.

Ralph Larmann studierte Schlagzeug mit dem Schwerpunkt Popularmusik am Rotterdams Conservatorium, bevor er sich 1991 überwiegend der Fotografie und dem Journalismus zuwandte. Seit 1992 designt und produziert Ralph Larmann hochwertige Bildbände, Konzertbroschüren und Ausstellungskataloge für Unternehmen und unterschiedlichste Künstler aus der Welt der Rock- und Popmusik sowie der Klassik, seit 2000 mit seinem eigenen Full-Service-Unternehmen, der Ralph Larmann Company. Als freier Fotograf und Autor erstellt er für Unternehmen, Künstler, Lichtdesigner und Magazine aufwendige Foto- und Textdokumentationen auf nationalem und internationalem Parkett. Unzählige Stars und Events konnte Ralph Larmann seit 1989 in faszinierenden Fotografien festhalten. In der Ausstellung mit dem Titel „Die Kraft des Augenblicks – Konzert und Eventfotografie" präsentierte er in Zusammenarbeit mit Lightpower im Rahmen der Prolight+Sound 2007 und der Musikmesse 2007 eine Auswahl seines Gesamtwerkes im Großformat (245 cm x 170 cm) in der Galleria der Messe Frankfurt.

Ralph Larmann estudió percusión en el conservatorio de Róterdam especializándose en música popular, antes de dedicarse desde 1991 a la fotografía y al periodismo. Desde 1992, diseña y produce magníficos libros ilustrados, prospectos de conciertos y catálogos de exposiciones para empresas y diversos artistas del mundo de la música rock, pop y también clásica. Desde el año 2000 lo hace con su propia empresa de servicios integrales, la Ralph Larmann Company. Como fotógrafo y autor independiente realiza suntuosas documentaciones a base de fotografías y texto para la platea nacional e internacional. Desde 1989, Ralph Larmann ha tenido oportunidad de captar fascinantes fotografías de incontables estrellas y eventos. En la exposición titulada «Die Kraft des Augenblicks – Konzert und Eventfotografie» (la fuerza del instante – fotografía de conciertos y eventos), presentó en colaboración con Lightpower y en el marco de la Prolight+Sound 2007 una selección de la totalidad de su obra en gran formato (245 x 170 cm) en la galería de la Feria de Exposiciones de Fráncfort.

Ralph Larmann a étudié la batterie (orientation musique populaire) au Conservatoire de Rotterdam, avant de se consacrer principalement à la photographie et au journalisme en 1991. Depuis 1992, il conçoit et produit des ouvrages illustrés de qualité, des brochures de concerts et des catalogues d'expositions pour des entreprises et des artistes on ne peut plus divers, issus du monde de la musique pop/rock, mais aussi de la musique classique. Depuis 2000, il exerce cette activité au sein de sa propre entreprise «full service», la Ralph Larmann Company. Photographe et auteur indé-pendant, il élabore des documentations, notamment photographiques, très complètes pour des entreprises, des artistes, des créateurs de lumière et des magazines de la scène nationale et internationale. Depuis 1989, il a réalisé d'innombrables et fascinants clichés de stars et d'événements. L'exposition intitulée «Die Kraft des Augenblicks – Konzert und Eventfotografie» (La force de l'instant – la photographie de concert et événementielle), organisée en collaboration avec Lightpower dans le cadre du Salon Prolight+Sound 2007 et de la Musikmesse 2007 (le plus grand salon européen des instruments de musique et des matériels, logiciels, éditions et accessoires musicaux), a permis au public de découvrir, à la « Galleria » de ce salon de Francfort, une sélection grand format (245 cm x 170 cm) de ses œuvres complètes.

Ralph Larmann ha studiato percussioni specializzandosi in musica popolare presso il Conservatorio di Rotterdam, prima di dedicarsi, nel 1991, alla fotografia e al giornalismo. Dal 1992 Ralph Larmann ha progettato e realizzato volumi illustrati, dépliant di concerti e cataloghi di mostre di alto livello per imprese e artisti del mondo della musica rock, pop e classica, a partire dal 2000 con la sua società full service, la Ralph Larmann Company. In qualità di fotografo e autore produce documentazioni fotografiche e testuali per aziende, artisti, light designer e riviste di livello nazionale e internazionale. Innumerevoli celebrità ed eventi sono stati immortalati nelle affascinanti fotografie di Ralph Larmann sin dal 1989. L'esposizione "Die Kraft des Augenblicks – Konzert- und Eventfotografie" (La forza dell'istante – fotografie di concerti ed eventi), realizzata in collaborazione con Lightpower in occasione della Prolight+Sound 2007 e della Fiera della musica del 2007, permette di ammirare una selezione delle sue opere in grande formato (245 cm x 170 cm) presso la Galleria della Fiera di Francoforte.

www.larmann.com
www.stagedesign.org

CREDITS

THEATER

Conception and Direction: Heiner Goebbels
Scenography and Lighting: Klaus Grünberg
Dramaturgy: Stephan Buchberger | Live-Video:
Bruno Deville | Costume Designer: Florence von
Gerkan | Actors: André Wilms and the Mondri-
aan Kwartet | Date of Performance: 10/19/2006
and 10/20/2006 Location: Grand Théâtre, Lux-
embourg, Luxembourg | Producer: Théâtre Vidy-
Lausanne E. T. E. | Co-Producers: Schauspiel
Frankfurt (German premiere), Spielzeiteuropa/Ber-
liner Festspiele, Pour-cent Culturel Migros, T&M-
Odéon Théâtre de l'Europe, Festival d'Autonome
Paris, Wiener Festwochen/With the friendly as-
sistance of the foundation "Landis & Gyr"/spon-
sored by "Programme Culture 2000" (Union de
Théâtres de l'Europe UTE, Résau Varèse)

Production: phase7 performing.arts, Forum Neu-
es Musiktheater of the Stuttgart State Opera
Art Director: Sven Sören Beyer | Concept:
Sven Sören Beyer and Christiane Neudecker
Costume Design: Pedro Richter/ Sabine Hahn
Lighting Design: Sven Nichterlein and Sven
Sören Beyer | Softwareart: Frieder Weiß | Tech-
nical Director phase7: Sven Nichterlein | Date of
Production: 03/18/2005 – 03/20/2005 | Loca-
tion: "Forum Neues Musik-theater" at Stuttgart
State Opera

with the Ensemble Modern, the German Cham-
ber Choir, the actor David Bennent and the
Baritone Georg Nigl | Music & Direction: Heiner
Goebbels | Scenography and Lighting: Klaus
Grünberg | Costumes: Florence von Gerkan
Assistant Director: Stephan Buchberger | Pre-
miere Opera Geneve, October 2002 | Copro-
duction of Berliner Festspiele, Festspielhaus
St. Pölten, la Filature-Scène nationale de Mul-
house, Ensemble Modern, Kulturstiftung Deut-
sche Bank, Fondation fédérale pour la culture

OPERAS

Director: Dorothée Schaeffer | Production Man-
agement: Philipp Köppl | Concept and Set Design:
Florian Kradolfer | Lighting Design: Reinhold Müller
Date of Production: 01/26/2007 and 01/28/2007
Location: Lech am Arlberg, Schlegelkopfplatz

Producer: Premium Classics GmbH | Director:
Zhang Yimou | Project Manager: Tobias Kühnel
from Show Plan | Conductor: Maestro Janos Ács
Orchestra & Choir: Orchestra et Coro Opera
Giuseppe Verdi di Salerno | Choreography and
Executive Director: Chen Weiya | Set Design:
Gao Guangjian | Set Design, Costumes and Req-
uisites: Zeng Li | Lighting Design: Sha Xiaolan
Setting: Nüssli GmbH | Lighting Equipment and
Video Equipment: ETF Procon France | Date of
Production: 07/09/2005 | Location: VELTINS-
Arena, Schalke/Gelsenkirchen

Producer: Bregenzer Festspiele GmbH | Direc-
tor: Robert Carsen | Set Design: Paul Steinberg
Lighting Design: Patrick Woodroffe | Date of Pro-
duction: 07/20/2006 – 08/19/2006 | Location:
Water Stage Bregenz, Austria

Organizer: Erfurt Theater in Cooperation with
the City of Erfurt | Technical Director of Erfurt
Theater: Dr. Stefan Ritter | Overall Director: Gen-
eral Manager Guy Montavon | Musical Director:
Walter E. Gugerbauer | Production: Werner Her-
zog | Stage Design: Maurizio Balò | Costumes:
Franz Blumauer | Lighting Design: Vincenzo Rap-
oni | Overall Technical Direction and Realization
of Sound, Lighting and Video: Neumann & Müller
Veranstaltungstechnik Dresden | Executive Pro-
ducer: Jörg Bernhardt | Sound Director: Helge
Petzold | Sound Design/FOH-Crew: Omar Sam-
houn, Robby Höhne | Lighting Crew Chief: Thomas
Landgräber | Date of Production: 08/10/2002

Location: "Domplatz", Erfurt

MUSICALS

Producer: Stage Entertainment GmbH | Direc-
tor/Costume Design/Mask & Puppet Co-Design/
Additional Lyrics: Julie Taymor | Scenic Design:
Richard Hudson | Lighting Design: Donald Holder
Mask & Puppet Design: Michael Curry | Year:
2007 | Location: "Theater im Hafen", Hamburg

Producer and Impresario: Michael Brenner | Ex-
ecutive Producer: Dagmar Windisch | Script and
Direction: Ben Elton | Production Designer and
Video Director: Mark Fisher | Lighting Design-
er and Video Director: Willie Williams | Sound
Designer: Bobby Aitken | Costume Designer:
Tim Goodchild | Choreographer: Arlene Phillips
Technical Production Supervision: Andreas Re-
scheneder, Ted Irvin | Year of Production: 2004
Location: Musical Dome, Cologne, Germany

Producers: Thomas Krauth, Andrea Friedrichs/
Starlight Express GmbH | Director: Dion McHugh
Artistic Director: Steven Rosso | Set Design and
Costumes: John Napier | Lighting Design: David
Hersey | Lighting Design Assistants: Rick Belzer,
Douglas Cox | Year of Production: 2007 | Loca-
tion: Bochum Theater

Producers: Jeffrey Seller, Robyn Goodman, Kevin
McCollum, Live Nation, Roy Miller, Dan Markley,
Ruth Hendel/Danzansky Partners, Jam Theatricals
Associate Producers: Sonny Everett, Mariano
Tolentino, Jr. | Director: Walter Bobbie | Set
Design: Anna Louizos | Lighting Design: Ken
Billington | Year of Production: 2006 | Location: Colo-
nial Theatre in Boston & Imperial Theater in New York

CONCERT TOURINGS

Eurovision Song Contest 2007   306

Executive Producer: Heikki Seppälä | Event Manager: Kjell Ekholm | Show Producer: Ilkka Talasranta | TV Producer: Tapani Parm | TV Director: Timo Suomi | Assistant Director: Heido Kokki | Lighting and Screens Designer: Mikki Kunttu | Stage Designers: Jenni Viitanen, Kalle Ahonen, Samuli Laine, Kristian Schmidt | Production Designer: Riikka Kytönen | Technical Managers: Matti Helkamaa (Audio), Kaj Flood, Ossian Kyrklund | Lighting & Sound Equipment: Spectra Stage & Event Technologies (general contractor), Eastway Sound & Lighting Oy | Lighting Consoles Equipment: MA Lighting International GmbH Equipment Intercom Configuration: Riedel Communications | Date of Production: 05/10/2007 and 05/12/2007 Location: Helsinki Arena, Helsinki, Finland

SPECIAL EVENTS

Opening Ceremony of the 15th Asian Games 320

Producer and Artistic Director: David Atkins from David Atkins Enterprises on behalf of the Doha Asian Games Organizing Committee (DAGOC) Lighting Designers: Fabrice Kebour, Andrew Doig Associate Lighting Designer: Steve Shipman Lighting Equipment: Bytecraft Entertainment Pty Ltd. (chief supplier) in co-operation with Procon Event Engineering GmbH | Network Manager (lighting): Paul Collison | Production Manager (lighting): Jamie Henson | Lighting Programmers: Jim Beagley, Romain Labat, Roger Ray, Maran Persoons | Project Manager (Bytecraft): Paul Rigby Crew Supervisor (Bytecraft): Mat Burden | Crew Chief (Bytecraft): Gary Senior | Crew Chief (Bytecraft): Andreas Knaak | Data Network Design (Bytecraft): Murray Taylor | Senior Production Electrician: Philby Lewis | Production Electricians: Chris Nicholls, Stu Cochrane, Nigel Holbrough, Nicholas Reeves, Craig Maroun | Scenic Lighting Supervisors: David Brown, Stephen O'Keeffe Scenic Electricians: John Dutton, Craig Knight, Suzanne Brooks, David Lee, Mark Wotton | Field of Play Electricians: Nic Coulson, Bill Paton, Jonathan Young | Senior Lighting Desk Ops: Romain Labat, Maran Persoons, Roger Rey | Followspot Caller: Prem Scholte Albers | Date of Production: 12/01/2006 – 12/15/2006 | Location: Aspire in Doha, Qatar

SkyArena Frankfurt – Overture to the 2006 FIFA World Cup Germany™   338

Client: Tourismus+Congress GmbH Frankfurt am Main | Idea, Concept and Production: Atelier Markgraph GmbH (AM) | Creative Direction: Roland Lambrette (AM), Stefan Weil (AM) | Art Direction: Alexander Hanowski (AM) | Director: Titus Georgi, Philipp Stölzl | Lighting Design: Gunther Hecker Musical Composition: Parviz Mir-Ali | Motion Design & Photoproduction: Martin Retschitzegger, Maria Johanna Ochsenhofer, Markus Egerter, Holger Mayer | Project Manager: Isa Rekkab (AM) Assistants of the Project Manager: Andreas Behl (AM), Tim Wender (AM) | Editorial Staff: Andreas Siemer (AM), Birgit Joest (AM), Martin Maria Schwarz, Matthias Schäfer | Technical Directors: Roger Nientiet (AM), Barbara Ackermann (AM) Graphics Production: Zinnecker-Werbestudio GmbH Audio Visual Equipment: XXL-Vision Medientechnik GmbH | Sound Equipment: Media Spektrum GmbH & Co. KG | Lighting Equipment: Satis&Fy AG Deutschland | Radio Engineering: MM Communications | Projection Towers: Nüssli (Deutschland) GmbH | Facade Applications: Marburger Dienstleistungen/Kletter-Spezial-Einheit | Music Production: Meirelli O.S.T. GmbH | Music Recordings: hr-Sinfonieorchester, hr-Bigband | Construction Management: Andreas Sieberg (AM) Production Manager (Software and Live-Act): Kim Krier (AM) | Year of Production: June 2006 Location: Frankfurt/Main

XX. World Youth Day 2005   350

Producer: WJT gGmbH | General contractors for event, building and construction services: Bilfinger Berger AG, Abteilung Hochbau Köln, HSG Technischer Service GmbH | Setting: StageCo Deutschland GmbH | Lighting Concept: rgb studio für lichtgestaltung GmbH | Lighting Equipment: Procon Event Engineering GmbH | Video- & Projections-Suppliers: ARGE, CT Germany, XL Video Sound Suppliers: ARGE, Crystal Sound, Neumann & Müller GmbH, Sirius AG | Year of Production: 2005 | Location: "Marienfeld" near Cologne, Germany

Blue Goals   358

Lighting Design: Michael Batz | Lighting Equipment: Procon Event Engineering GmbH, Philips Licht Deutschland, BOCATEC Video- and Lasertechnik GmbH | Year of Production: 2006 | Location: Hamburg

Afrika! Afrika!   364

Initiator: André Heller | Planning: André Heller (initiator), Rolf M. Engel (outside paintings, exhibitions at the foyer, substructures corporate design), Matthias Hoffmann | Producer: Matthias Hoffmann/Afrikanische Zirkus GmbH & Co. KG Set Design: Günter Jäckle and Friederike ("Fritze") Krauch | Lighting Design: Günter Jäckle | Lighting Equipment: SHOWTEC GmbH | Years of Production: 2006/2007 | Locations: Hamburg City Park/"Gummersbacher Straße", Cologne-Deutz, Germany

Symphony Of Light at Berlin's central station   376

Producer: Deutsche Bahn AG | Overall Concept: Sebastian Turner (Strategic Planning), Thomas Krecker (Agency Producer)/Scholz & Friends Lighting Design: Jerry Appelt | Lighting & Audio Equipment: Procon Event Engineering GmbH Equipment Pyrotechnics: Flash Art GmbH, The Show And Effects Company | Laserequipment: Omicron Laserage Laserprodukte GmbH | Technical Realization: Jan Thommen 360 Grad | Date of Production: 05/26/2006 | Location: Berlin Central Station

ACKNOWLEDGEMENT

Thank you very much:

Céline Gaudier, Barbara Suthoff, Sven-Sören Beyer (phase7), Christiane Neudecker (phase7), Norbert Ommer, Babette Karner, Axel Renner, Tobias Kühnel (Showplan), Alex Ostermeier (Neumann & Müller GmbH), Natali Frisch (Disneys DER KÖNIG DER LÖWEN Theater im Hafen Produktionsgesellschaft mbH), Nils Lunow (Stage Entertainment Germany), Britta Larmann, Ulrike Wingenfelder (BB Promotion), Christina Lück (BB Promotion), Susanne Krämer, Ellen Lübke-Meier (Starlight Express GmbH), Sam Rudy, Brig Berney, Ken Billington, Anna Louizos, Willie Williams, Mark Fisher, Ken Watts, Lisa Johnson, Scott Holthaus, Ralph-Jörg Wezorke (Lightpower/MA), Tom Bilson (Stageco group), Oliver Schlossarek (StageCo Germany GmbH), Werner Herbst (StageCo Germany GmbH), Tony Gittins, Lee Chateris, Fraser Elisha, Blue Leach, Denis Papin (XL Video GmbH), Hans-Jürgen "Lauti" Lautenfeld (Trend Event), Jake Berry, Dale Skjerseth, Wob Roberts, Manfred Meyer, Morten Carlsson (PROCON MultiMedia AG), Udo Willburger (PROCON PROCON Event Engineering GmbH), Sven Siekmann (PROCON MultiMedia AG), Jana Wohlien (PROCON MultiMedia AG), Jörg Przyborowski (PROCON Event Engineering GmbH), Marco Niedermeier (A&O Lighting Technology GmbH), Jerry Appelt, Werner Kimmig, Jan Thommen (360 GRAD), Manfred "Ollie" Olma (mo2), Mikki Kunttu, Tapani Parm, Heikki Seppälä, Marcus Krömer, Edelgard Marquard (Sennheiser electronic GmbH & Co. KG), Heinke Hahn (Sennheiser electronic GmbH & Co. KG), Michael Casper-Blunck, Stephen Found (BYTECRAFT Entertainment), Angela Kratz (Atelier Markgraph GmbH), Gunther Hecker, Mike Brockmann (rgb studio für lichtgestaltung gmbh), Günter Jäckle, Hans Otto Richter and Markus Katterle (Flash Art GmbH).
My very special thanks to Bettina and Philipp Larmann for believing in my work.

© 2007 daab
cologne   london   new york

published and distributed worldwide by
daab gmbh
friesenstr. 50
d - 50670 köln

p + 49 - 221 - 913 927 0
f   + 49 - 221 - 913 927 20

mail@daab-online.com
www.daab-online.com

publisher ralf daab
rdaab@daab-online.com

creative director feyyaz
mail@feyyaz.com

edited & written by ralph larmann
© photos by ralph larmann
page 391 reinhard langschied
ralph larmann company
www.larmann.com

layout, imaging & pre-press alexandra faber
editorial assistant natalia cristina l. javier
ralph larmann company
www.rlcompany.de

english translation ingo wagener
spanish translation concha dueso
french translation yannick van belleghem
italian translation chiara pagnani
german text copy-editing silke martin
translations and copy-editing by zoratti studio editoriale
www.studio-editoriale.com

printed in poland by ctp ozgraf

isbn 978-3-86654-032-3